Discerning Eyes

Viewers on Violence

Julie Firmstone

UNIVERSITY
OF LUTON

press

British Library Cataloguing in Publication Data
A catalogue record for this book is available from the British Library

ISBN: 1 86020 565 8

Published by
University of Luton Press
University of Luton
75 Castle Street
Luton
Bedfordshire LU1 3AJ
United Kingdom

Tel: +44 (0)1582 743297; Fax: +44 (0)1582 743298
e-mail: ulp@luton.ac.uk
www.ulp.org.uk

Cover Design by Gary Gravatt
Typeset in Van Dijck MT and Helvetica
Printed in Great Britain by Thanet Press, Margate, Kent.

Contents

For my parents Pat and Michael Firmstone

Acknowledgements

Without the financial support of the Broadcasting Standards Commission this book would not have been possible. Special thanks go to Andrea Millwood Hargrave, Research Director of the Commission, whose idea it was to bring together all the recent research in the area of audience perceptions of violence. Her friendly support and encouragement throughout the project was much appreciated. Special thanks go to Professor David Morrison, Research Director of the Institute, who not only read through the manuscript and gave me valuable advice, but also provided me with endless encouragement. Michael Svennevig, Research Director of the Research Centre for Future Communications at the Institute, also deserves thanks for his support and guidance. I would also like to thank Professor Manuel Alvarado for his editorial assistance and general enthusiasm for the review. I am also grateful for the help and the professionalism of the staff at the ITC library. One of the pleasures of this project was meeting and talking with Professor James Halloran. I feel especially grateful and honoured that he has made such a valuable contribution to the book and would like to thank him. Finally, I would like to thank Simon Walker for his constant support and encouragement.

Preface

Perhaps more than most other branches of the social sciences, communications research has always, at a fairly direct level, been intertwined with politics. One reason for this is that the performance of the media in all societies is seen as political. After all, the performance of the media contributes to the ways in which we view and come to understand the world, and the media play an important role in political and social agenda setting.

It was felt that it would be valuable therefore to situate the studies presented in this book within some kind of historical framework so that the reader has an appreciation of the politics of the research field. Given the substantial influence of funding on the nature and direction of research, it was considered that an examination of the financial support that has assisted the development of mass communications research in Britain would be worthwhile. In what way have research councils, governments, policy organisations and the media industry contributed to the manner in which communications research, and more specifically research into media violence, has developed? By providing explanations it is hoped to give the reader insights into the politics within which research has evolved. For this reason, Professor James D. Halloran was approached to contribute a contextual historical essay on the development of British mass communications research. I am pleased to say he agreed to take on this task. His contribution is presented as a foreword to the main review of research studies. It is hoped that Professor Halloran's discourse will allow the reader to place the studies of audience perceptions of violence presented by Julie Firmstone as an outcome not only of communications research history, but as a social product produced by an apparently never-ending political concern with violence in society.

Professor Manuel Alvarado
May 2002

3

Foreword

Factors influencing the emergence and early directions of mass communication research in Great Britain

James D. Halloran

At a recent conference on the Corruption of Academic Science held by the Council for Academic Freedom and Academic Standards, it was emphasised that in the present climate in higher education, with its economic problems and its many assessments and evaluations, academics and institutions were increasingly desperate to 'get their hands on money so that they could pursue their research'. There was also 'a feeling that, because of this, the balance of power between commercial organisations and universities had shifted', leaving the universities as a junior partner, with academic freedom threatened and publication restricted. Government was also in a powerful position, for whatever the universities and researchers might want to do, government can and does exert effective control through the purse strings.

David Triesman, general secretary of the Association of University Teachers, accepted the need for cooperation, 'but not at the price of academic freedom and independence'. He felt that the intensity of the pressures on universities to secure research funding posed a serious threat to their integrity, and that a clear set of ethical guidelines was required to ensure that academics could contribute their expertise without compromising their scholarly standards.

It may be more marked now in a crude economic sense but, in principle, was it ever any different? It is over a quarter of a century ago that Horowitz (Horowitz, 1968), commenting on independent and autonomous research, saw such research as seriously threatened when linked to policy – media, commercial or governmental, particularly if funded from these sources.

The history of mass communication theory and research has received more attention in recent years, but much of the present literature on the subject stresses the evolution of ideas that influence the field, rather than the ways in which the social context of the day helped shape these ideas. As a result there has been relatively little inquiry into the sources of institutional and financial support for mass communication research during the years that it crystallized into a distinct field of inquiry. In what follows this important aspect of developments in the field will not be ignored.

We need to recognise that any research, including research into the communication process and the mass media, can be and has been influenced by many factors. These might range from government and media policies through the needs of the market place and expressions of social concern, to the state of the disciplines employed in the research. An attempt will be made in these pages to provide specific examples of the factors that influenced the development and direction of mass communication research in one specific country, Great Britain.

The way in which research is influenced will differ from country to country, different combinations of factors applying in different places. Additionally, the situation is far better documented in some places than in others, so our knowledge is not evenly distributed. Nevertheless, the same general principle applies in all cases, namely that no research is free from some form of constraint, direct or indirect, and its development and operations must be studied within the wider historical, political, and social contexts.

Mass communication research does not have a long history, and this is particularly true in Great Britain. If we focus on the disciplined, systematic, social scientific approach to the study of the media as social institutions and communication as a social process (admittedly, not the only approach), then in Great Britain the research story does not really start until the early 1960s.

The first general review of the field undertaken in Great Britain, and published in 1963 (Halloran, 1963) was able to refer to very few research exercises, and these concentrated on effects from a social psychological standpoint and/or were associated with the market and media institutions. The few general books published by British sociologists ignored the subject, and references to 'media' and 'communication' were not even to be found in the index in these books. University teachers such as Richard Hoggart and Raymond Williams were writing and asking pertinent questions, but the subject was not formally taught in universities. It would appear that the first course on this country on the sociology of the mass media was provided by the Extra-Mural Department of Leicester University in 1962.

It is also worth noting in this connection that the Committee on Broadcasting (the Pilkington Committee), when it reported in 1962 (HMSO, 1962), confined its remarks on research to two paragraphs, and these were not particularly informative or relevant with regard to the understanding of broadcasting, still less to the understanding of the communication process.

In November 1961 the Home Secretary, responding to expressions of concern about the alleged harmful influence of television, held a conference of representatives of religious, educational, social service and other interests to discuss juvenile delinquency and, in particular, the extent to which the incidence of delinquency derived from the general state of society. Arising from this conference the Independent Television Authority (ITA) offered to finance research into the impact of television on society, with particular reference to its effect on young people – the hope, although not directly expressed, being that it would be established that there were no adverse effects stemming from television.

Following discussions with the ITA and the British Broadcasting Corporation (BBC), the government arranged, as a first step, for a group of experts in the fields of psychology, sociology, social studies and statistics to hold a conference. This conference recommended, *inter alia*, that research should be carried out, but that it should not be primarily concerned with the direct study of the effect of television on delinquency. It was felt that the scope should be wider and should deal with the part that television plays, or could play, in relation to other influences in communicating knowledge and fostering attitudes. The conference also recommended that a committee should be set up to give further consideration to the whole problem, to initiate and coordinate research, and to administer the funds that were made available.

The Vice-Chancellor of the University of Leicester accepted the Home Secretary's invitation to become Chairman of this committee, and in July 1963 the committee had its first meeting, and began its work with the following terms of reference:

> To initiate and coordinate research into the part which television plays, or could play, in relation to other influences, as a medium of communication and in fostering attitudes, with particular reference to the ways in which young people's moral concepts and attitudes develop, and on the process of perception through which they are influenced by television and other media of communication, and to administer any funds made available for such research.

Although the committee was appointed by the Home Secretary and, strangely enough, was responsible to the Prison Department (the association of television with crime and delinquency), the government was unable to provide for its servicing because it was clear that a secretary would be required who was familiar with the media and with research in mass communications. Neither the ITA nor the BBC could meet this need or, more importantly, the need for independence, so the chairman invited a member of the staff of his own university, a sociologist who was familiar with and had published work in the field of mass communication, to become secretary of the committee.

It was originally envisaged that, after an initial period of discussion and negotiations with researchers, the committee would make contracts for research and then spend a relatively quiet time awaiting the outcome of the commissioned research before making any public statement. Although under no specific obligation to produce a formal report, or make recommendations – its main task was to coordinate and initiate research – the committee was expected to arrange for the publication of research reports and, where appropriate, to comment on the findings.

However, when the committee had surveyed the research interests and the plans of social scientists in Great Britain it found that very few of them were working on research topics which related to its terms of reference, even when these were widely interpreted. A number of proposals were received but, with one exception, these were judged to be unlikely to contribute substantially to an understanding of the problem area.

The publication (Halloran, 1963), which had led to the appointment of the secretary of the committee, consisted of 'a study of the mass media and their challenge', particularly attention being given to the validity of the claims about media influence – positive and negative – in the light of systematic research. The book, based on articles written in 1962 was published in 1963, and inevitably contained few references to British *research*. Neither the base from which to construct a research strategy, nor the researchers capable of executing a strategy were available in Great Britain.

The committee, therefore, decided that it would have to proceed slowly, clarifying by its own interpretation of work in other countries, particularly in the USA, both the significance of the terms of reference and its own ultimate objectives. It would have to identify the problem areas amenable to social scientific research, assessing the social relevance of the specific questions that could be formulated within these areas, seeing what methods, skills and resources were available and could be used in attempts to answer these questions, and then finally establishing its research priorities.

It was fortunate for the future of mass communication research that the committee recognised that it had been presented with an unusual opportunity to promote social scientific research in a relatively new, fascinating and important area in which fact and objectivity were urgently required to inform an increasingly spirited, yet ill-informed public debate. In the circumstances the committee soon saw that it would be a mistake to dissipate this opportunity by premature decisions to commission the first proposals put forward. To confine its activity to the acceptance and rejection of research proposals was not desirable when the substantial expertise and experience of the members could be directed to the creation of a sound base-line for future research at a much more comprehensive level.

The importance of this committee, its policy and strategy, in the development of mass communication research in Great Britain and beyond cannot be over-estimated (Television Research Committee, 1966). Its decisions led to the establishment at the University of Leicester in 1966 of the first independent institutional base for mass communication research in the country and, for quite a number of years after that, Leicester led the field in research innovations and publications. It is worth noting that the terms of reference given to the Leicester Centre by the Television Research Committee were considerably wider than those given to the committee by the Home Office. The committee made a conscious decision to go beyond what some saw as its crime and delinquency remit, which it regarded as far too narrow and restrictive. Needless to say, this was not welcomed by some of those who had expressed the concern in the first place, and were looking to research to show that their fears were justified.

The policy adopted by the committee enabled the Centre to develop a comprehensive, sociologically oriented research policy at national and international levels, in which the media as social institutions, and communication as a social process were studied within the wider social context.

So, with regard to the factors influencing research – which is really an aspect of the sociology of knowledge, how knowledge is obtained – the important point to note is that the first major development in mass communication research in Britain, which later was to have far-reaching international implications, had its origins in a range of circumstances, including social concern, the response to that concern by both the government and the media (including the provision of funds), the composition of the committee set up by the government, the servicing of that committee and the policy it adopted, and the state of the art of communication research and its contributory disciplines at the time.

Two further points need to be emphasised. First, that although this is a single specific example of research development – unique at one level: a case study in fact – the general principles are universally applicable. Second, that in this particular case the implications of this development, stemming from the policy adopted and the aforementioned circumstances, go beyond research policies, programmes, projects and publications. The Leicester Centre became the headquarters of the International Association for Mass Communication Research, which now has some 2,000 members in over seventy different countries. As a result of this Centre staff became involved in numerous international research exercises and acted as consultants to academic, media and political bodies. Students from all over the world studied at the Centre, and ex-students and staff hold prominent positions in academia and the media in many countries.

In a social scientific exercise we need to recognise how all this came to pass. We also need to recognise that attempts to deal with the history of mass communication research at times seem more intent on slotting events into neat post-hoc constructed categories, representing some value position, than in dealing with what actually happened. What actually happened is rarely as neat and tidy and as amenable to categorisation, particularly to dichotomisation, as some who write about it seem to think.

As already indicated, the Television Research Committee did not find it possible to construct a research strategy and programme from the base that was available in Great Britain. Not surprisingly, therefore, it turned to the United States, where research into the media and communications had a longer history, in order to see what research had been done and what might be learned from it with regard to the committee's remit.

The research situation in the USA at the time, as interpreted by the Secretary of the Committee, was presented as a major part of a working paper which went a long way to determining the research policy and strategy of the Committee (Halloran, 1964). Inevitably, the bulk of the research reviewed fell within the mainstream of mass communication research in the USA, which has been referred to as 'conventional research'. At the risk of oversimplification, in broad, general terms, this research would claim to be value free, with positivistic, empiricist, behaviouristic, psychological emphases.

Although this type of research was reviewed rather critically in the report, care was taken not to throw the baby out with the bath water, for there was much useful work that fell under the abovementioned headings. It was also made clear that critical comments on this type of work should not be seen as a rejection of rigorous methods, experimental work, or quantification. It was essentially a matter of emphasis and balance. There was, however, a severe criticism of the primacy of this position of 'scientism', where 'scientific' was defined solely or mainly in terms of method, and where little or no attention was given to theory, concepts or the nature of the relevant substantive issues and their relationship to wider societal concerns.

In short, in the USA mass communication research had developed, like other branches of social science, essentially as a response to the requirements of modern industrial, urban society for empirical, quantitative, policy-related information about its operations. Most of the research that was carried out was geared to improving the effectiveness and profitability of the media, often regarded simply as objects of study, or as neutral tools in achieving stated aims and objectives, usually of a commercial nature. This was at the heart of administrative or service research, where the emphasis was on improving methods to facilitate the achievement of specific goals rather than on refining concepts, developing theories, challenging systems or achieving social change.

In this way the prevailing research mode, although often referred to as abstracted empiricism, was certainly not abstracted from the society within which it operated, and which it was geared to serve. With this in mind the report to the Television Research Committee argued that it was necessary to ask about the questions which had not been asked as well as those questions which had been asked. For, in what was a media rather than a societal centred approach in mainstream, conventional communication research, theory had been neglected, conceptualisation was crude, content analysis superficial, and the media were not seen in relation to other institutions. There were few, if any, questions about power, policy, organisation and control; little reference to structural considerations, and rarely were attempts made to study the social meaning of the media in historical or sociological contexts. Overall the bulk of the research was unbalanced, tending to concentrate on one aspect of the process (effects and reactions), to the neglect of the factors that influenced what was produced.

This dominant research approach was marked by an emphasis on answers seen to be useful in the short term, a concentration on methods (particularly on what could be measured, with its false notion of precision), and a focus on the individual with the related confinement of the notion of media influence to imitation and attitude and opinion change. The possible influence of the media on institutions, in defining social reality, in setting the social-political agenda, in legitimating certain forms of behaviour and institutional arrangements, and on cultural change tended to be ignored. This, so it was argued in the report, produced a completely inadequate understanding of the communication process, the notion of media influence and the role of the media in society. Moreover, sometimes research results were little more than artefacts of the research design and the false conceptualisations employed (Halloran, 1964 & 1970).

Reliability (the replication and confirmation of results) was regarded as much more important than validity (whether results actually dealt with the phenomenon they claimed to be dealing with) and, in some cases, the availability of accepted methods even determined the nature of the problem to be researched. This led to a plethora of allegedly definitive statistical statements about the trivial, inconsequential, and at times plainly invalid (Halloran, 1981).

It would, of course, be quite unfair and indeed inaccurate to suggest that up to the early 60s there was no communication research in the USA that fell outside the mainstream, conventional parameters outlined above. Hanno Hardt (Hardt, 1992) provides a corrective historical perspective when, starting by reminding us that the issues of communication and society figured prominently in the work of the Chicago pragmatic sociologists well before the second world war, he goes on to review the work of such as Park, Blumer, Wirth, Sapir, Lasswell, Westley, MacLean, Lazarsfeld, the Frankfurt School, Gerbner, Janowitz, Rosenberg, Manning-White and others who addressed wider issues in those early days and who, although not sharing a common approach, could not immediately or readily be placed within the dominant aforementioned conventional parameters.

On the other hand, Hardt also reminds us that these interests in the wider social and cultural aspects of media and communications remained in the margins. They were never taken on board by mainstream communication researchers, where the approach of Wilbur Schramm (Schramm, 1954) with its close links to journalism education predominated.

Schramm's interest was journalistic rather than scientific, although he had an interest in methodological issues as they related to practical questions.

However, there was no apparent interest in producing a theoretical framework for the critical assessment of the media in American society.

Moreover, a review of the sociological textbooks in use at the time in the USA indicated that the study of the media and mass communication did not figure prominently in the sociological syllabuses of the day. There were some individual exceptions but, on the whole, this field of study had not attracted the work of social theorists. It had been hived off to Schools of Journalism and Schools of Communication.

Commenting on the emergence of a new interdisciplinary field, which was becoming known as 'communication research', Dallas Smythe saw the new researchers as consciously adopting the stance of 'scientism'. Consequently, 'the evidence from the fields of history, sociology, political science and economics were ignored as being unfit for acceptance as science' (Smythe, 1954).

It is also worth noting that even some of those, like Lazarsfeld, who grappled with the problems posed by the conflict between critical and theoretical interests on the one hand, and empirical demands on the other, never really escaped from an attachment to the commercial interests of the culture industry, and the political concerns of government. In a sense 'critical' was seen as within the limits of the status quo, and consequently the type of critical challenge referred to later, and the associated theoretical concerns, never really surfaced in sustained research programmes (Hardt, 1992; Gitlin, 1978; Katz, 1987).

Concluding his excellent coverage of research approaches in the period which ended just before the Television Research Committee in Great Britain was given its terms of reference, Hardt (1992) maintained that in the USA:

> mainstream communication and media research had failed to address critical developments from without its boundaries. It had remained within specified categories of interests reflected in an academic specialisation in the study of communication that was interdisciplinary by its commitment to a behavioural science orientation, but without any significant or successful attempt to break out of its monadic circle.

Attention might usefully be drawn to the background of Wilbur Schramm, who is generally regarded as one or the fathers, if not *the* father, of the establishment and institutionalisation of mass communication research in the United States.

It is important to emphasise Schramm's role as a psychological warfare contractor, operator and promoter. It is recognised that his 'personal income and professional prestige were to a significant degree dependent upon his work for the US Air Force, US Information Agency, Department of Defence and the CIA-sponsored propaganda organisation Radio Free Europe' (Simpson, 1994). Nor was Schramm the only father with such a background. Simpson states that at least six of the most important US centres of communication studies had a similar background, and relied heavily on government funding. This gave communication studies in the United States its base, its form and its direction.

In these pages we need not question the politics or morality of this, but it is important to recognise its significance in influencing, if not determining, what type of research is carried out, what questions are asked, what becomes defined as 'good research', who are rewarded and who are ignored or even penalised, who become the accepted authorities; in fact, how communication itself is defined and understood.

Of course, the sources of research funding and their needs are not the only factors to be taken in to account in examining the development of research, but in this particular case they do account for a great deal in determining the establishment, nature and direction of mass communication research in the United States. They also go some way towards explaining why certain macro, critical and challenging questions were not asked, at least within the mainstream of conventional research. This despite an earlier, if somewhat peripheral interest in such questions.

Moreover, this type of conventional research was not confined to the United States. It was exported far and wide, becoming the accepted approach in some countries. It was clearly reflected in some research in this country (Hilde Himmelweit was not uninfluenced by Schramm), but it never became dominant or institutionalised.

The funding picture in the United States was certainly not repeated here, either in intention or scale. Nevertheless, it would be a mistake to think that, because the picture is not so clear and blatant as in the USA, external factors, including the sources of funds, played no part in the development of mass communication research in this country.

In the mid 1960s, the Television Research Committee in Great Britain was introduced to a vast body of work from the USA, most of it serving special political, commercial and media interests rather than questioning or challenging. Thousands of projects had been carried out in a fragmentary, ad hoc, piecemeal fashion, but there was little evidence of the systematic accumulation and development of a corpus of knowledge, and few attempts to relate the work to an appropriate social theory or critique of society.

As far as the Television Research Committee was concerned it could be said that the main outcome of this review of the state of the art in mass communication research in the early 60s was that at least it was known what not to do – a great step forward – but that there was still the task of deciding precisely what to do in terms of formulating research policies and strategies, and deciding on the appropriate supporting structures.

With regard to research policies and strategies the Television Research Committee, in its final report in 1969, drew attention to the following (Television Research Committee, 1969):

(a) It is important to study the media and mass communication not as isolated phenomena, but as integral parts of a wider social system.

(b) There is a need for theoretical as well as methodological developments in the study of mass communication, and for integration and coordination of research efforts.

(c) It is necessary to develop interdisciplinary work with a view to producing comprehensive research strategies with sufficient power to capture all the relevant processes in a given problem area.

(d) Little research has as yet been carried out into the role of the mass media in the early stages of the child's development. Attempts should be made to remedy this, and long-term developmental studies should also be undertaken.

(e) It is desirable to carry out further research into the positive as well as into the negative aspects of the media and to ask questions about the potential of the media, for example about how they could be used in broadening or developing taste, increasing social participation, improving international understanding, or reducing prejudice.

(f) Research should include studies of the production process. Our research has shown that it is important to know how media producers (the term is used in the widest sense) see their role, and to have information about their values, attitudes, aims, conventions, intentions, working conditions and general background. Patterns of recruitment should also be examined.

(g) The products of the mass media, and therefore the effects, depend (at least in part) on the prevailing system of ownership, control and support. Research (on a wider, interdisciplinary plane covering economic, legal and political aspects) should investigate the relationships between programming and control. The planning of programme schedules and the allocation of time and money to different types of programme are but two aspects of this problem area which our own research has shown require further and closer examination.

(h) In studying the influence of the media on social attitudes and values, researchers should not be deterred by the difficulties and complexities of the problem from carrying out investigations along a wider front than one normally finds in mass communication research. Questions should be asked about the influence of different forms of presentation of news, current affairs and political issues. Media content should be examined for values, omissions as well as commissions should be studied, the question of trivialisation and the possibility that the media are working against instead of in support of an active 'participatory' democracy, should not fall outside the scope of a comprehensive research policy.

In terms of the development of research and the factors facilitating this, the most important thing to note about these recommendations was that, as far as can be ascertained, they represented the first ever formal statement of research policies which sought to challenge rather than to serve, and which aimed to replace the hitherto prevailing narrow, psychological approaches with a broader, critical, sociological orientation. That this represented a change in the direction of mass communication research in Great Britain – 'a break in the field' – was recognised by Stuart Hall (from the cultural studies approach) when he reviewed *The Effects of Television* (Halloran, ed, 1970). 'Halloran's introductory essay and his major contribution, "The Social Effects of Television" are both model exercises in revisionism – a breakout from the theoretical and ideological restraints of previous research frameworks ... a break in the field and all the more welcome for that' (Hall, 1970).

Commenting further on a specific research exercise from Leicester, *Demonstrations and Communication* (Halloran *et al*, 1970), he wrote, 'This study avoids both the traditional definitions of the field which operate in standard media/political studies, and also the extreme position which makes the media the prime sources of violence. By restoring the historical and political context the study pinpoints the amplifying and labelling role of the media – *it looks remarkably like a break in the field*' (Hall, 1970).

But what happened to these recommendations? A starting point for this focus might be a UK British Film Institute (BFI) and Social Science Research Council (SSRC)-sponsored conference, 'Representations in the Mass Media', in April 1983. The past two decades of research were reviewed and the considerable intellectual developments of the period were acknowledged. However, the emphasis was still on what had not been accomplished, and what ought to be done in the future. Significantly the way ahead, as mapped out, had much in common with the report by the Home Office Television Research Committee, which was passed on to the Social Science Research Council in 1969.

At that time, responding to the recommendations of the Television Research Committee, the SSRC, through one of its panels, suggested that specialised research centres should serve as focal points for research where training, consultation, research expertise, and knowledge about a special topic would be readily available. It was further recommended by the SSRC panel that it was to centres such as these to which the government and others could initially look for the development of the research necessary for the establishment of a sound basis for public policy in the development and use of mass communication media.

The panel also reinforced the Committee's proposals for close cooperation between broadcasters and researchers, with the media providing funding and facilities, but they should not control, nor unduly influence.

What did the SSRC do about this? Very little of a concrete nature, although some eight years after the special panel's report another advisory panel was set up (May 1978). This reported in June 1980, but neither this report, nor the report of the special panel, appear to have been distributed outside the confines of the SSRC. What is more to the point is that, judging from the 1980 report, this panel was not even aware of the earlier report of the Television Research Committee, nor of the earlier panel's reactions to it!

One contribution of this panel was to point out that in nine years (1970-1979) the SSRC had spent under £300,000 on mass communication research out of a total research expenditure of £25 million. In 1968 the Television Research Committee estimated that, in any one year, 60 times more money was spent on commercial/media research (not including advertising research) than on basic mass communication research, and in 1974/75 the Annan Committee estimated that, in one year, £1.25 million was spent by the BBC and IBA on ratings research.

Some time after the panel reported a small group was formed by the SSRC, but met only once, and the emphasis appeared to be on meetings and conferences rather than on research. This is hardly an impressive record, and certainly not one likely to attract collaborators and financial supporters.

It may be argued that in more recent years the SSRC's successor, the ESRC, in a somewhat differently defined and wider field, went some way to redressing the earlier shortcomings. However, Bill Melody, who was in charge of the implementation of these initiatives, still found it necessary as recently as 1990, in his article in *InterMedia*, to focus on the public interest, and on the policies that would meet public interest requirements and other democratic criteria in the anticipated future. He also suggested ways in which more attention could be given to those public interest implications, hitherto neglected, and emphasised the importance of attempting to make good our lack of knowledge by an increased research effort. "We need research which would provide an overall systematic analysis of the long term implications of technological developments and associated institutional changes" (Melody, 1990). One must agree, whilst sadly reflecting that these are almost the same words (certainly identical sentiments) to those in the UNESCO working paper and the Television Research Committee's report of 20 years before.

The SSRC/BFI 1983 conference also focused on broadcaster/researcher cooperation. Thirteen years earlier a much more high-powered conference, on the same theme, attended by top flight researchers and broadcasters from all over the world, including the heads of broadcasting from several countries, was held in Leicester. The SSRC contributed to this conference, its officers participated in it, and it received the widely disseminated report, which contained several recommendations for research and broadcaster/researcher cooperation (Halloran and Gurevitch eds, 1971).

The relationship between broadcasters and researchers is crucial to the development of mass communication research. Often we hear from broadcasters that research must be 'practical, relevant and easily understood'.

But this can never be the sole consideration, for it would equate the good of the media with the good of society.

The main problem lies with research which does not work within media frameworks, but which starts from communications/societal needs which question and challenge the existing set-up and suggests alternative possibilities. As things stand it is difficult, if not impossible, to obtain media support for this type of critical research.

When research is related to policy we are confronted with a problem with regard to the autonomy and independence of social science in problem-solving situations. If we maintain that a main aim of research is to contribute to making society a better place to live in, then social problems should be addressed without identifying with established order values. But, on the whole, independence is inversely related to influence in decision-making.

By the late 1960s in Great Britain, the pioneering Television Research Committee was no longer alone in its opposition to conventional research. In its search for new ways of exploration it had been joined by other forces and traditions – for example, by Raymond Williams and by the Birmingham Centre, with Richard Hoggart and Stuart Hall – in what became known as 'critical research,' although this term was never precisely defined, and was often inaccurately opposed to what was termed pluralism. However, the institutional infrastructure was barely visible, and systematic social scientific research was still pretty thin on the ground.

Just as it can be misleading to generalise about conventional mass communication research, it is even more misleading to do so about the critical approach which, although owing much more to European thought and scholarship than the conventional approach, nevertheless reflected the influence of American sociology. For example, the writings of the Rileys which, although not leading directly to any specific research projects in the USA, facilitated the introduction into research strategies of concepts such as social structure, process, social systems, reference groups, conditions of production and structural dependency. This played no small part in the formulation of the above recommendations by the Television Research Committee (Riley & Riley, 1959).

It could be argued that the main unity of the critical approach – if in fact a unity could be identified at that time – was in its opposition to conventional work rather than in any shared, more positive approach with regard to the future of the media in this country. For the critical umbrella covered a variety of positions, and it could be that some of the more extreme ideological positions should not really be classified as social scientific research.

In taking a closer look at the critical, problem and policy-oriented research, primarily with a sociological perspective, it should be noted here that a distinction may be made between policy-oriented research and policy research. The latter, as we have seen (Hardt, 1992) generally seeks to bring about the efficient execution of policy, and thereby make the existing system more efficient. On the whole, it is not concerned to ask questions about the validity of the system, or to challenge predominant values or suggest alternatives. Policy-oriented research, on the other hand, ideally addresses itself to the major issues of our time, and is concerned, amongst other things, with questioning the values and claims of the system, applying independent criteria, suggesting alternatives with regard to both means and ends, and exploring the possibility of new forms and structures (Halloran, 1981).

It is not necessary to make an either/or issue out of these different approaches. We are not talking about incompatibilities, but about the different implications for policy and society of approaches which prevailed in the past (and which, up to a point, are still with us) and those which emerged in the sixties and seventies (Blumler 1981, Gitlin 1978). Put crudely, and to repeat, the conventional approaches of the past which characterised so much communication research, explicitly or implicitly, served and supported rather than criticised or challenged.

It was appreciated that to talk in terms of a critical, problem and policy-oriented, sociological approach may beg more questions than it answers. There are different sociological approaches, and it might be said for example, that sociological functionalism may have more in common with psychological functionalism than it has with the other, more critical sociological approaches (Riley & Riley, 1959; Hardt, 1992).

There is some truth in this but, even so, it could still be maintained, with the qualifications that follow later, that there is something meaningful and distinctive about the critical sociological perspective referred to above, and most definitely something that marked it off from the approaches that prevailed in the past. The sociological perspective and the concepts that come with it at least *make it possible* to adopt a more holistic, challenging attitude to the status quo.

The decision to take this line was influenced by the fact that this developing, critical thrust was seen not only as offering the greatest contrast and challenge to the older approaches, but also as providing a major contribution to the most important international debate on vital communication issues which developed in the 1970s. Its advocates and practitioners played no small part in the development of mass communication research in Europe (particularly in Britain), and it was also influential internationally, particularly through UNESCO policies, research and publications where, at least for a time, it supplanted the earlier, conventional approach associated with Wilbur Schramm and his colleagues (Halloran, 1981; UNESCO, 1971).

Additionally critical research, although stemming from a wide range of positions and reflecting different values, was seen as less likely than conventional research to be encumbered by historical and institutional relationships with journalism and broadcasting. Moreover, it was not as closely linked with markets, audiences and publics, and was less inclined to have a service, administrative or commercial character. Needless to say, such research was not without its value implications, but at that time it was seen as likely to be more independent of the institutions it was studying.

As far as the study of media institutions is concerned, the approach was more likely to be from the outside, with a critical policy or problem orientation. The Leicester study on the media coverage of the anti-involvement in Vietnam demonstration was a good example of this (Halloran *et al*, 1970).

Critical research does not ignore problems central to the media, but ideally it never takes these problems as defined by media practitioners or politicians. Ideally, its starting points are the major social issues of our time, as defined from declared theoretical or value positions, not necessarily the major media issues as narrowly defined by the professionals, owners or policy-makers.

At the risk of over-simplification, the main social scientific characteristics of this critical approach which, although with diverse earlier roots, emerged in the late 60s and 70s may be summarised as follows. First and foremost is that it dealt with communication as a social process; secondly, that it studied media institutions not in isolation, but together with other institutions, and within the wider social context (nationally and internationally); and thirdly, that it conceptualised research in terms of structure, organisation, professional-isation, socialisation and participation.

One of the clear implications of this is that the status quo, the existing system, was not taken as sacrosanct, and that all aspects of the communication process should be studied. The factors (historical, economic, political, organisational, technological, professional, personal, etc) which impinge on the production process and determine what is produced demand close scrutiny as well as those which influence how what is produced is used. In the past the emphasis in research was on use, reaction, effects, influence, etc and not on ownership, policy, control, structure, organisation and production relationships (Halloran 1981; Curran & Gurevitch 1993).

We need to ask how do policies and strategies lead to research programmes and projects? It is one thing to formulate research policies and strategies, but it is altogether another thing to operationalise these in the shape of research programmes and projects, and it is yet another thing to obtain the supporting funds for such research, particularly if the research has a critical edge to it. But this is the context of research. This is social reality.

In the late 1960s and the 1970s quite a number of projects were designed, executed and reported on at the Leicester Centre (established by the Television Research Committee in 1966) which, in a variety of ways, reflected the aforementioned critical thrust as well as the circumscriptions. It is also important to note that this was possible because, at the Centre, a firm funded base had been established, with a reasonably broad remit and a fair degree of autonomy.

Demonstrations and Communication (Halloran *et al*, 1970b) reported critical research which covered the whole communication process, including the factors, which governed the production of news. *Racism and the Mass Media* (Hartmann & Husband, 1974) examined the role of the media with regard to racial prejudice. The alleged relationship between television and delinquency was critically addressed (Halloran *et al*, 1970c) in a study involving over three hundred delinquents. The role of the school in relation to the mass media was also studied (Murdock *et al*, 1976), as was television production (Elliott 1972, Tracey 1977, Halloran 1977, Murdock 1977). *Media and Development* (Golding 1974 and 1977, Hartmann 1978) extended the critical research to the international level. In addition, this whole programme was supported by a wide range of theoretical, methodological and political papers, as well as by contributions to international conferences, and the provision of consultancies to media, academic and international institutions such as UNESCO (Halloran, 1981 and 1990).

By the mid 1970s critical research was on the map in Great Britain. Not all of it came from Leicester; for example, Birmingham was very active in the field of cultural studies, but at that time the bulk of it (ie research projects actually carried out) did. Generally, research in Great Britain was developing rapidly, but by no means all of it could easily be classified as critical nor, one suspects, would most of those involved have wished it to be so classified (Blumler 1981).

It is possible that the developments and changes are best illustrated by looking at the different ways in which specific issues were addressed by the different approaches. The best example in this connection, amply demonstrating both the weaknesses of the conventional approach and the broader, more realistic perspectives of the sociological approach, is to be found in research which attempted to deal with the alleged media/violence relationship.

At the risk of oversimplification it may be said that the conventional approach, in addition to the many shortcomings previously outlined, was over media-centred (Halloran, 1980; Howitt & Cumberbatch, 1975). Its main (at times its sole) focus was violence on the screen (defined in numerous, and often extraordinary ways), rather than violence in society. True to the effects tradition, its main question was what do the media do to people? And this question was normally answered, sometimes in bizarre situations, via indications of imitation, modelling, increased aggressive drive, attitude change and similar individual reactions.

The sociological approach would turn the question around, so instead of asking 'what do the media do to people?' it would ask, What do people, differently situated in society, with different backgrounds, experiences, cultures, opportunities, associations, skills and competences make of what the media offer? Moreover, in keeping with its processual and societal underpinnings, it would also focus on media production and the various functions served by those productions. One important point to note is that when these sort of questions are asked entirely different research strategies are required; questions which take us away from the gross oversimplifications associated with an obsession with linear causality.

In examining this sociological approach with regard to the media and violence in some detail it must be emphasised that in research, as in the public debate, we are not dealing with a single phenomenon. Violence may be categorised in several ways – there is collective or political violence and personal or individual violence. Collective violence, seen from an historical perspective, is much more normal and historically rooted than is commonly accepted. Much of what we now accept as legitimate, even as laudable, stems from violent action in the past.

Violence is frequently thought of in terms of assassinations, murders, riots, demonstrations, assaults, robberies, rapes and acts of vandalism. In fact, for many, this sort of 'illegitimate' behaviour represents the totality of violence. But there are those who would include war, police behaviour, corporal and certainly capital punishment. A still broader definition might include poverty, deprivation, economic exploitation and discrimination. In this connection it should be noted that society may contribute to 'illegal' violence by the approval it gives to certain forms of 'legitimated' violence.

When violence is examined within the appropriate historical and cultural contexts it can be seen that it is culturally, and even sub-culturally defined. Some forms of violence are acceptable and approved; others are not. But the acceptance and approval usually depend more on the objective, the perpetrator and the victim than on the nature and form of the violent behaviour. Media policies and programmes, public attitudes to the media, and even research approaches reflect this. The roots of violent behaviour, as with the concept of violence itself, must also be studied within the appropriate national, historical, cultural and economic contexts. It is worth noting that few of those who have systematically and scientifically studied violent behaviour have cited the media as a major cause. The roots of such behaviour are usually found elsewhere in society. It was argued that the main task was to see whether the media related to violence *in any way*, and not just in the simple, direct causal ways of popular speculation. It is also worth noting in this respect that the media-centred, conventional researchers seemed to be totally unaware of the work of other scholars (psychiatrists, sociologists, criminologists, historians, legal scholars and political scientists). This is a good example of the isolation of so much mass communication research which was referred to earlier.

Although the roots of violent behaviour may not be the main concern of media researchers they cannot be ignored, and the media/violence relationship must be studied within a wider framework than is normally used. To adopt this approach is not to suggest that the media have no influence. However, it must be emphasised once more that in much of the conventional research the role of the media and the process of influence were not properly understood. The restriction of the notion of influence to imitation, copying, increased aggressive drive and attitude change prevented such an understanding.

Clearly, violence is not unrelated to frustration, even though the relationship is not necessarily a direct one. Consequently, we might ask what, if anything, do the media contribute to frustration in our society and, through this, to aggression and violence? The main values in a commercially oriented, industrialised, urban society, where advertising plays an important part in media operations and in the economy generally, will be related to the achievement of material prosperity, and much effort, time and money will be expended on the promotion of this. Advertising seeks to make people dissatisfied, and to stimulate them to want more, irrespective of their economic circumstances. There is much more emphasis in the media and elsewhere on materialistic goals than on the legitimate ways of achieving these goals. For the deprived sections of the community the daily stimulation could exacerbate feelings of frustration and discontent.

Of course, there are other agents of frustration in society, but it would be foolish to ignore the possibility that the media, in their presentation of materialistic norms and values (by the portrayal of affluent lifestyles as well as by advertising) may increase expectations unrealistically, aggravate existing problems and thereby contribute to frustration and aggression.

This, however, is not the sort of relationship people normally had in mind when they expressed concern about the media/violence relationship. The condemnation of media content is highly selective. Not even all forms of media violence are condemned, any more than are all forms of violent behaviour.

The sociological approach, then, encourages this kind of holistic critical thinking and, when applied to the study of news, offers an entirely different perspective on the role of the media in society (Halloran, 1990).

One of the breakthroughs in the late 1960s and 1970s was a recognition (at least in some quarters) that the process of media influence was more indirect, more complex, and perhaps even more far-reaching than was commonly realised.

Violence and deviant behaviour, particularly in their extreme forms, are extensively covered by the media in most Western societies, and another example of media influence may be seen in the way such media portrayals play a part in defining problems and in giving focus to public concern.

It is not unreasonable to hypothesise that what people take from the media might influence their views about the nature and extent of violence in society. There have been different interpretations of the available evidence, but the main point was to draw attention to one of the several ways in which the media may be related to public perceptions of violence behaviour.

This approach enables us to appreciate that the media help to set the social/political agenda. They select, organise, emphasise, define and amplify. They convey meanings and perspectives, offer solutions, associate certain groups with certain types of values and behaviour, create anxiety, and legitimate or justify the status quo and the prevailing systems of social control.

They provide 'the pictures of the world' that are available to us and, in turn, these pictures may structure our beliefs and possible modes of action. It is in terms of these possibilities that it was argued that we must examine the influence of the media.

The media, of course, do not work in isolation. The interactions between media experiences on the one hand, and non-media experiences on the other, which differ from issue to issue, from person to person, and from country to country must also be studied.

The media may set the agenda in a regular, ordered and predictable fashion. Choice and selectivity in attention, perception and interpretation are thereby circumscribed, but they are not eliminated. The media portrayal of a riot, for example, may assist in the dissemination of 'riot skills', may produce a reactionary backlash, or may encourage an increase in social awareness and responsibility, which could lead to ameliorative action. Certain meanings can be predominant in the presentation of the riot, but these are still susceptible to a selectivity which reflects, *inter alia*, personal and group experiences in a differentiated and stratified society.

It was emphasised that one of the reasons why the media operate as they do was because readers and viewers had to be won and kept. For the daily news media, persons and events (particularly negative ones) are the basic units. Events are more likely to be reported if they occur within the space of one day. A demonstration is a news event, but the development of the related political movement does not have the correct 'frequency'. Consequently, violence becomes directly related to the events in the streets, and this tends to exclude background, explanations and context. One of the first major projects undertaken by the Leicester Centre in 1968 on the media coverage of anti-Vietnam demonstrations in London provided most revealing illustrations of these points (Halloran *et al*, 1970b).

This orientation, which stems from the organisation of the news process, and its basic assumptions could lead in another context to stereotyping and to the association of certain groups with violence, as well as to the acceptance of violence as a legitimate way of dealing with problems or as a necessary form of retaliation. Perceptions derived from these presentations may even influence 'official' attitudes, so that they come to match the stereotypes. The interpretations of the problem are therefore reinforced, and all sides behave as 'expected' (Cohen *et al*, 1973).

One other consequence of this type of presentation could be to play down alternative conceptions of social order; the status quo of power and control is maintained, conflict and dissent being managed in the interest of the authorities.

It is said, particularly by those who favour a law-and-order stance, that the media offer support for the demonstrators and rioters by providing publicity, and that this may encourage disruptive behaviour. 'Copycat' behaviour cannot be ruled out, but there is no convincing evidence to support it. The presence of cameras may even reduce the likelihood of violence (Tumber, 1982).

The media have been seen as the enemy of the police, particularly when photographing police violence. But they have also been criticised by the demonstrators or strikers for being part of the establishment and for facilitating police identification. Incidentally, the position of the camera, more often behind police lines than not, is very important in creating a perspective.

The media have influence, then, but the degree to which a demonstration or riot becomes an effective method of communication depends on factors other than the media; the media may simply reinforce the contending positions.

In their research Hansen and Murdock (1985) attempted to move on from the simpler assumptions about the way the media relay or reproduce dominant ideology. They saw news as a field of continual conflict in which competing discourses struggled for publicity and legitimacy, and were transformed and worked on as they passed through the news-making process. However, according to this view, although there is no longer the same emphasis on predictability of news outcomes, the activation of the themes available from history and popular imagery in the production of news still leads to 'meaning' being fixed quite early in the reporting process. Moreover, it is fixed in such a way that riot is associated with crowd and against community and public. Political significance is thereby devalued.

The views from both 'right' (the insurgent's friend) and 'left' (an instrument of state) may be too simple to describe a complex situation. Non-news programmes, including non-fiction, are not subject to the conditions surrounding the news process. The news, and some other programmes, are relatively 'closed', generally favouring the 'official perspective'. But other programmes may be more 'open' so that alternative views are presented. Consequently, there is scope for meanings to be negotiated from what is made available at any given time. But, as research on televising terrorism (Schlesinger *et al*, 1983) showed, this diversity was limited both in terms of what was available and the use that was made of this. Consequently, although the situation was not quite as closed as some would claim, the negotiations are inevitably confined within restrictive frameworks.

The likelihood was, then, that (even allowing for this 'openness') the media, and television in particular, in portraying disturbances will reinforce the simplistic analyses of complex situations, and this could lead – not directly by copying, but indirectly in relation to implied solutions – to an exacerbation of the situation. It is certainly not likely to lead to an increased understanding of the social situations which gave rise to the disturbances.

Generally, media violence is viewed negatively. There was the possibility that the portrayal of violence may serve a 'positive' function (at least from one standpoint) by acting as an instrument of social control and maintaining the status quo. The media coverage of violence may also enhance normative consensus and community depend on the media for most of their information. The media inform, create awareness, redefine the boundaries of what is acceptable and structure perceptions of the nature and extent of violence. In doing this they may bring people together in opposition to disorder, reinforce a belief in common values, facilitate the imposition of sanctions, and strengthen social control. But in order to do this the violence must be made visible throughout society – hence the importance of the media.

Although many of the hypotheses which stem from this approach have still to be put to the test, there is nothing new in the views which regard coverage of crime and violence as creating a sense of solidarity within the community by arousing moral concern.

There is, of course, much more to critical mass communication research than violence and news. The above illustrations of the media/violence relationship and news have been deliberately selected because they deal with issues which are at the centre of public debate, which have been intensively and extensively researched, and which provide the most significant examples of the differences between the conventional and critical sociological approaches.

Research – certainly the research that is actually carried out – is not just a matter of ideas, theories and methods. As noted earlier, research may be influenced by many factors; some research may be encouraged and other research discouraged or prevented. Obstacles are often put in the way of certain types of research, and it is important to note the questions that have not been asked (or funded) as well as those that have. These are obstacles external to social science (eg political, commercial, professional) although these are not entirely separate from the internal obstacles – ie the nature of social science with its discontinuities, lack of consensus and overt disagreements.

We might ask: what is progress? On this score it should be clear by now that progress is regarded here in terms of the development of a critical, sociological approach to the media and the communication process an approach which challenges rather than serves but, of course, this would not be everyone's idea of progress (McQuail, 1994).

Still, using these criteria it is possible to claim that, at least in the realm of ideas, definition of the field and questions asked, considerable progress has been made in mass communication research over the past 30 years. Nevertheless, it is important to remember with regard to research expenditure that the amount of research actually carried out, and the number of publications throughout the field, that the conventional approach is still very much in evidence.

In fact, at the level of research actually carried out, it might appear that progress is not so obvious. The agendas at conferences and meetings in the 1990s prompted a feeling of *déjà vu*, for they were not markedly different from those in the seventies in terms of the lists of *'what we ought to do in the future'*, and this is particularly so when we deal with the application of research to policy.

Attention was first drawn to one aspect of this problem nearly thirty years ago: "What Do We Need To Know – Are We Going To Be Allowed To Find Out?" (Halloran, 1973) For even if social scientists agree on what ought to be done, there is no guarantee that they will be allowed to do it. The question: Are we going to be allowed to find out? is as problematic today as it was a quarter of a century ago – perhaps even more so. We must ask why it is still necessary to call for an increased research effort in order to answer the questions that were first articulated years ago, and that have been on the agenda ever since. There is plenty of research activity today – but what sort of questions are being asked? What is being 'allowed' – funded?

The main focus of what has been written in these pages has been on the emergence – 'the breakthrough' – of a particular social scientific approach to research into the communication process and media institutions. There are other approaches, both within social science and outside it, which are not included. An attempt to provide a systematic, disciplined study of the nature and direction of research in recent years, and in the contemporary situation, is beyond the remit of this contribution. Nevertheless, it is worth noting that there are those who consider that, despite the burgeoning of research in recent years, on the whole the agenda is now geared to serving rather than to criticising, challenging or suggesting alternatives. For example, there are several instances of broadcaster/researcher cooperation which, on the surface, might seem to meet the recommendations of the Television Research Committee. However, closer inspection would appear to indicate that the cooperation is very much on terms decided by the broadcasters and other media practitioners. Similarly, with certain funding bodies, research is supported if it fits in with the needs and policies of those bodies. Has the wheel gone full circle?

Earlier, reference was made to what Horowitz wrote over thirty years ago about independence and policy research. Reference was also made to more recent expressions of concern by the Council for Academic Freedom and Academic Standards about autonomy, independence and cooperation in the current situation, with regard to university funding in this country. More recently still, we have been warned by Dr Peter Cotgreave, Director of Save British Science, of the dangers of government policy with its insistence on corporate involvement in academic funding.

According to Cotgreave there is a clear possibility 'that no one believes any more that any research is independent'[1] and that there is a widespread, although erroneous, belief in official quarters that 'blue skies research' is too vague and uncommercial. Moreover it is suggested that, because of the pressures, fewer and fewer academics are prepared to criticise or independently evaluate research or policy.

Although these comments refer mainly to the natural and physical sciences, there is no reason to believe that they do not apply, mutatis mutandis, to the social sciences, and to mass communication research in particular. In fact David Miller, from the University of Stirling Media Group, is highly critical of the way communication and media research is conducted in the UK. 'It's not just corporations that fund research which is to their commercial advantage. Most publicly funded research contracts contain clauses that enable government departments (and some other funding bodies – watchdogs, for example) not to publish anything they don't like, though it rarely comes to that. In most cases academics know what's required and don't investigate the more difficult areas (blue skies research, or critical research as described earlier) or, if they do, they fudge the answers and adjust their findings to what they feel will fly'[2] – and thus pave the way for another grant.

There are several ways in which researchers seek to rationalise their position, including an escape into 'methodological perfection'. Critical research, as they define it, may be confined to a criticism of methods without an appreciation that methods, important though they are, can never be more than a means to an end. But this stance enables the end to be ignored, or never defined.

Some may regard the above as overstatements, accepting that in the present circumstances it is inevitable anyway – perhaps even desirable! Whilst repeating that the intention here is not to carry out a disciplined survey of the current situation, I know from my own experience in mass communication research over 40 years that things are not quite what they used to be. Blue skies research – in our field I equate this with critical research – is not much in evidence today, and the overall research effort is now far more circumscribed.

The main point in commenting on the recent and contemporary situation in this way is to contrast it with the past, more particularly with a period which lasted no more than two decades, from the late 1960s onwards. This period is regarded by some (those who share critical values) as the halcyon days of mass communication research – the years of the 'breakthroughs'. They would question whether any real progress (apart from the proliferation of research exercises – many of them of dubious quality) in terms of questions asked, theories, methods and breakthroughs have been made since that time.

It was noted earlier that the Television Research Committee, and even the first panel convened by the ESRC to examine the recommendations of the Committee, no doubt recognising the discontinuities, differences and even conflicts existing within social science, called for the establishment of several institutions that could represent different approaches to the study of communication and the media. The Committee used approximately half the funds available to it to establish the Leicester Centre but, in keeping with its recommendations, it also attempted to support developments in other institutions. Grants were awarded to the Department of Sociology at Aberdeen University, to Dr Hilde Himmelweit at the London School of Economics (well known for her pioneering work), and to Professor Richard Hoggart at the University of Birmingham.

The outcome was not particularly encouraging, and could be seen as confirming the earlier suspicions of the Committee that, in this country, neither the researchers nor the structures were in place to enable the Committee to fulfil this part of its remit. Only the grant to Birmingham bore fruit. Although no doubt pleased to receive a grant, the Birmingham Centre would have flourished without it. It had its teething troubles and problems, but it had a reasonably sound base within the University from which it could operate and develop.

For reasons which never became clear (probably individual culpability) nothing came from the Aberdeen investment, and the grant to Dr Himmelweit surprisingly was not used. After a time the Television Research Committee decided to transfer this grant to Dr Blumler at the University of Leeds.

At one level Leeds had been first in the field. The Television Research Unit, based on a fellowship provided by Granada, had completed research projects under the direction of Dr I. Trenaman on further education programmes, and on the television coverage of an election, before the establishment of the Television Research Committee. Further election studies were carried out, but developments were slow to take place, and Dr Blumler, who succeeded Dr Trenaman, approached the Television Research Committee for support. It would appear that, at that time, the Television Research Unit at Leeds was regarded essentially as a unit – a somewhat marginal unit – peripheral to the University, which seemed reluctant to guarantee long-term support. It was some years before it became more firmly established within the University, and was able to fulfil the role that the Television Research Committee had in mind when it called for the establishment of several research institutions. The grant from the Television Research Committee may have helped it to survive.

The situation at Leicester was very different, and clearly this was not unconnected with the fact that the Vice-Chancellor of the University was chairman of the Television Research Committee, and that the secretary of that Committee became the first Director of the Centre for Mass Communication Research at the University. The grant from the Television Research Committee sustained the Centre for its first five years, although the University also made substantial contributions throughout this period. At the end of this period the Centre became an integral part of the University, benefiting considerably from its full support.

The advantages of this cannot be overstated. The initial grant, the University support, the freedom from external constraints and the relative security and permanence (some of those appointed at the outset remained active at the Centre for nearly 20 years) enabled the Centre to expand from its firm base, and obtain substantial additional research funds from media organisations and a wide range of funding bodies in many different countries. The Centre became recognised internationally as a 'centre of excellence' and was the headquarters of the International Association for Mass Communication Research for 18 years from 1972. But it really did have a head start, and was well supported.

It should also be emphasised that in those early days the research funds usually came without any strings being attached. The total atmosphere was different from the current one. In fact, at that time the University Research Board at Leicester, which had overall responsibility for the acceptance and administration of all research funds from external sources, would not readily accept any restrictions or qualifications.

But things have changed; in fact they were beginning to change some time before the development of current policies and economic pressures. In the 1960s media organisations and institutions, whether through self-preservation (reactions to government enquiries) or through a mixture of ignorance and arrogance, offered some cooperation to academic researchers. It was possible to detect at the BBC, particularly after Pilkington, a feeling that the Corporation was bound to be shown in a favourable light by academic research. This attitude changed, however, when some of the early critical research, which questioned and challenged existing policies, structures and practices, failed to meet such confident expectations. Cooperation on our terms only and if the research results are likely to be 'useful', gradually became the order of the day.

Of course it was and still is possible to adopt a critical stance, without such cooperation or external funding. But even 'desk research' requires a firm base and a degree of permanence and autonomy, which, these days, is not always in evidence.

There is also the question of credibility. Inevitably there will be a reluctance to accept where evidence is eschewed and substantiation not considered necessary. Few will listen, and fewer still will take notice or be influenced. This could have unfortunate implications. Power may corrupt, but powerlessness corrupts absolutely, as those who are ignored and fail to find an audience, or have influence only within a narrow circle, may take refuge in an intellectual or even a pseudo-intellectual ghetto where they speak to and write for each other – a sort of incestuous graveyard.

But where does all this leave us? What can we learn from the emergence and development of mass communication research in this country over the last half century?

It all depends on what we mean by mass communication research; what we want from it, what we consider to be its main aims and objectives. If we wish it to serve the system, to reinforce media and, even these days, government policies as carried out by funding councils, then mass communication research may prosper, as it did in the past in the USA, for example. In fact there are those who would consider this to be its legitimate function – its only *raison d'être*. But if one wishes to stand outside the system to criticise, challenge and suggest alternatives, to have broader societal considerations in mind rather than confirm and comply, to have genuine freedom and autonomy, which should be at the heart of academic activity, then a different base is required – a firm, secure base where researchers have autonomy and some degree of permanence, and are not dependent on short-term grants based on the perceived immediate needs of the media, the government or funding agencies.

We may conclude as we began by recalling what Horowitz had to say so, many years ago. "Where policy needs rule the critical effort will be the exception rather than the rule, and the deterioration in the quality of social science will be inevitable – the utility of social science to policy making bodies depends on the maintenance of some degree of separation between policy making and social science" (Horowitz, 1968). Is it not obvious that this is a major feature of the short history of mass communication research in this country?

References

Blumler, J. (1981) 'Mass Communication Research in Europe', in Wilhoit, G.C. and de Bock, H. eds, *Mass Communication Review Yearbook*, pp.37-49, Beverley Hills and London: Sage.

Cohen, S. and Young, J. eds. (1973) *The Manufacture of News*, London: Constable.

Curran, J. and Gurevitch, M. eds. (1993) *Mass Media and Society*, London: Edward Arnold.

Elliott, P. (1972) *The Making of a Television Series*, London: Constable.

Gitlin, T. (1978) 'Media Sociology: The Dominant Paradigm', in *Theory and Society*, Vol 6, pp.205-253.

Golding, P. (1974) 'Media Role in National Development', *Journal of Communication*, Vol 24, No.3, pp.39-53.

Golding, P. and Elliott, P. (1977) *Making the News*, London: Longman. Hall, S. (1970) Watching the Box, *New Society*, pp.295-296.

Halloran, J.D. (1963) *Control or Consent?* London: Sheed and Ward.

Halloran, J .D. (1964) *The Effects of Mass Communication*, Leicester: Leicester University Press.

Halloran, J.D. (1970a) *Mass Media in Society: The Need of Research*, Paris, UNESCO Reports and Papers on Mass Communication, No.59.

Halloran, J.D, Elliott, P. and Murdock, G. (1970b) *Demonstrations and Communication: A Case Study;* Hammondsworth: Penguin.

Halloran, J.D, Brown, R. and Chaney, D. (1970c) *Television and Delinquency*, Leicester: Leicester University Press.

Halloran, J.D. (1973) 'Research in Forbidden Territory', in Gerbner, G, Gross, S.P, and Melody, W.H. *Communication Technology and Social Policy: Understanding the New Cultural Revolution*, pp. 547-553, London: Wiley & Son.

Halloran, J.D. and Gurevitch, M. (1971) *Broadcaster/Researcher Cooperation in Mass Communication Research*, Centre for Mass Communication Research, University of Leicester.

Halloran, J.D. (1977) 'An Explanatory Study of Some Factors that Influence the Production of Drama in an Independent Television Company in the United

Kingdom', in *Organisation and Structure of Fiction Production in Television*, Torino, Editizione RAI, pp. 9-50, Italian and French translations pp.51-140.

Halloran, J.D. (1978) 'Social Research in Broadcasting: Further Developments or Turning the Clock Back?' *Journal of Communication*, Vol 28, No.2, pp.120-132.

Halloran, J.D. (1981) 'The Context of Mass Communication Research', in McAllnany, E, Schnitmann, T. and Janus, N.Z, eds, *Communication and Social Structure: Critical Studies in Mass Media Research*, pp.21- 57, New York: Praeger.

Halloran, J .D .(1990) *A Quarter of a Century of Prix Jeunesse Research*, Munich: Stiftung Prix Jeunesse.

Halloran, J.D. (1990) 'Mass Media and Violence', in Bluglass, R. and Bowden, P. eds, *Principles and Practice of Forensic Psychiatry*, pp.511- 575, London: Churchill Livingstone.

Halloran, J.D. (1991) 'Mass Communication Research – Obstacles to Progress', *InterMedia*, IIC, Vol 19, Nos 4-5, p.23.

Hansen, A. and Murdock, G. (1985) *Constructing the Crowd: Populist Discourse and Press Presentation*, London.

Hardt, H. (1992) 'On Ignoring History: Mass Communication Research and the Critique of Society', in *Critical Communication Studies: Communication, History and Theory in America*, pp.77-122, London: Routledge.

Hartmann, P. and Husband, C. (1974) *Racism and Mass Media*, London, Davis Poynter.

Hartmann, P. (1978) 'Cultural Identity and Media Dependence', in *WACC Journal*, XXV, No 1, pp.2-5.

H.M.S.O.(1962) *Report of the Committee on Broadcasting* 1960,CMND No 1753, London.

Horowitz, I.L.(1968) *Professing Sociology*, London: Aldine Publishing Co.

Howitt, D. and Cumberbatch, G. (1975) *Mass Media, Violence and Society*, London: Elek.

Katz, E. (1987) 'Communication Research Since Lazarsfeld', *Public Opinion Quarterly*, Vol 51, pp.525-545.

McQuail, D. (1994) *Mass Communication Theory: An Introduction*, (third edition), London: Sage.

Melody, W.H. (1990) 'The Information in IT – Where Lies the Public Interest?' *InterMedia*, Vol18, No.23, pp.10-18.

Murdock, G. (1977) 'Fabricating Fictions: Approaches to the Study of Television Drama Production', in *Organization and Creativity in Television*, Turin Edizioni, RAI, pp.181-198. Italian and French translations, pp.141-180.

Murdock, G. and Phelps, G. (1976) *Mass Media and the Secondary School*, London: Macmillan.

Riley, J .W. and Riley, M.W.(1959) 'Mass Communication and the Social System', in Merton, R.K. ed, *Sociology Today – Problems and Prospects*, New York: Basic Books, pp.569-578.

Schlesinger, P, Murdock, G. and Elliott, P. (1983) *Televising Terrorism: Political Violence in Popular Culture*, London: Comedia.

Schramm, W. ed, (1954) *The Process and Effects of Mass Communication*, Urbana, Illinois: University of Illinois Press.

Simpson, C., (1994) *Science of Coercion. Communication Research and Psychological Warfare* 1945-1960, Oxford University Press.

Smythe, D. (1954) 'Some Observations on Communication Theory', *Audio Visual Communication Review*, Vol 12, pp.24-27.

Television Research Committee, (1969), *Problems of Television Research*, Leicester: Leicester University Press.

Tracey, M. (1977) *The Production of Political Television*, London: Routledge & Kegan Paul.

Tumber, H. (1982) *Television and the Riots*, London: BFI Publishing.

UNESCO (1971) *Proposals for an International Programme of Communication Research*, Paris: COM/MD 20.

Notes

1   Quoted in 'The Plot Thickens: Does corporate cash taint research?' by John Crace in *The Guardian* (Education), 12 February 2002, pp10-11.
2   ibid.

Introduction

This book presents a review of research findings on the audience's perception of violence on television over the last two decades. It has its origins in a paper prepared for a seminar on 'Violence and the Domestic Screen', presented by the Broadcasting Standards Council to the 'Joint Working Party on Violence', which was set up in 1997 to address public concern about violence on television. The working party consisted of senior figures from the BBC, BSC, and Independent Television Commission. The original review has been augmented and built upon to provide an up-to-date overview of the literature in the area, focusing specifically on what the audience thinks about violence on television.

The selection of research reported on reflects the changes that have taken place in how the audience is viewed by researchers. Audience perception studies represent a departure from traditional effects studies in that they consider the audience as active rather than passive viewers. Whilst it falls outside the scope of this work to explore how the model of the viewer has been developed to take account of viewers' interactions with that which they see, it is necessary to explain the relationship between the two fields of research.

Perception studies of how viewers define violence, and of what they take violence to be, appear as a most welcome departure from the effects tradition. However, it is evident that the motivation for such research is rooted primarily in concern over the effects of media violence in society. The effects paradigm therefore remains as a major influence even if it is not followed. In part, this connection might be attributed to sources of funding, at least in the case of some of the studies presented. Although they of themselves are not predominantly interested in questions of effects, those who commissioned much of the research reviewed in this book nevertheless owe their political existence to concerns over the negative effects of television. In this respect, research into audience perceptions can be thought of as effects research at one level removed, or at least it could be seen to be so if viewed historically – see Professor Halloran's forewording essay. A case in point would be the exercise of measuring levels of violence on television through content analysis. The method is made much more sophisticated if violence is coded in line with viewers' empirical definitions of what is or is not violent, rather than measure that which is taken to have characteristics of what we objectively take to be violence. However, despite the increased sophistication afforded to content analysis when it is informed by perception studies, the question remains of why one wishes to score frequencies and levels of violence in programmes? The answer takes us back to concerns over the effects of violence. To this extent audience perception studies do not offer the departure from the effects paradigm that might at first be considered. The place of audience perceptions research within the effects debate can be judged from the research studies presented here, and I will return to this question in the final chapter. Crucially, the studies reviewed locate the viewer as a person, and explore the meanings that people bring to watching television.

Given this inextricable link between the two fields of research, I found it impractical not to include those studies relating to effects that I thought contributed to the central findings of the main literature search. However, as a general rule, studies belonging to the effects paradigm have not been covered, not least because comprehensive reviews relating to this literature already exist (Cumberbatch and Howitt, 1989; Freedman, 1984; Gauntlett, 1995; Livingstone, 1990; Potter, 1999). It should also be noted that although I have attempted a thorough analysis of the work in the area of the perceptions of violence, it is not the case that all work unearthed during the literature search has been reported upon. The main criterion used in selecting those for discussion has been the editorial one of pertinence and relevance to the main aim of the review. This has necessarily meant judgement on my part in terms of the quality of research and the substantive contribution to the issues addressed. Therefore, studies where the perception of violence is mentioned only in passing or where perceptions did not form the main focus of the research have generally been omitted. In reporting on the studies presented I have kept interpretation and commentary to a minimum, preferring instead to descriptively introduce this area of research.

Following Professor Halloran's forewording essay and this introduction, the subsequent two chapters cover those studies that have focused on adult viewers' perceptions of television violence. Chapter three reviews studies into perceptions of violence in factual television, and considers violence in the contexts of News, War News, Documentary and Crime Reconstruction programmes. At the end of this section there is a review of research that has explored the opinions and perceptions of violence by individuals who have survived a violent crime or a disaster. The fourth chapter considers what influence the context in which fictional violence occurs has on viewer's perceptions, and shows how genre affects viewer's interpretations of violence. Studies into the perceptions that children have about television violence are explored in chapter five. This research is considered under the headings of Realist Drama, Crime Reconstruction, Documentary, Fictional Television, and News programmes, allowing a comparison to be made with the findings of similar studies of adult perceptions of violence across the various genres. The sixth chapter aims to provide an overview of supplementary research findings that present the perceptions of several specific groups of viewers, and also presents findings of studies involving violence in video games. Finally, chapter seven gives a brief summary of research conducted in other countries that relates to the other studies reviewed.

.

1

Perceptions of violence in factual television

Since 1970 the Independent Television Commission (formerly the Independent Television Authority and the Independent Broadcasting Authority) has conducted an annual survey of public opinion on a range of broadcasting related topics. The results are issued annually in the Commission's publication *Television: the Public's View*.[1] Each year part of the survey addresses the issue of offence and acceptability. When asked 'are there any issues on television that cause you concern nowadays?', 40 per cent of survey respondents in 2001 said yes. When these respondents where then asked what issues caused them most concern, 20 per cent said violence, 18 per cent said swearing and offensive language, and 16 per cent said sex.[2] Concern about violence was reported equally by people of all ages, whilst fewer younger people and more older people were concerned about language and sex on television. Until 1995 the survey asked those respondents who had been offended by something what types of programmes were most likely to cause them offence.[3] Over several years the genre of Films, Comedy/Variety/Chat Shows and Popular Drama were consistently ranked most likely to cause offence, followed by News and Current Affairs and Drama Documentary. For example, in both 1992 and 1993 news and current affairs caused offence to 13 per cent of respondents.[4] In the same years offence was found in drama documentaries by 8 per cent and 6 per cent of people.[5] In 1995 news/factual programmes resulted in offence to 12 per cent of respondents. In 1994 Crime Reconstruction was added to the list of programmes with 4 per cent of people quoting them as a source of offence.[6] Answers varied according to programme genre when respondents were asked what exactly they had found offensive or unacceptable in a programme. In 1993 the most common complaints about news/current affairs programmes were the showing of dead or mutilated bodies, disturbing news items, intrusion into people's grief and suffering, too much detail or explicitness, and insufficient care over what is shown at times when children might be watching.[7] Famine and starving children, violence and sensationalism were also sources of dissatisfaction in other years. In 1992 the sources of offence in Drama Documentaries were violence, bad language, and sex. Crime Reconstruction programmes raised concerns about violence, the encouragement of copycat crimes, and about the content being of an excessively realistic or frightening nature. It is not possible to report figures for more recent years since this line of enquiry was not pursued.

Following a similar remit to that of the ITC, the Broadcasting Standards Commission (formerly the Broadcasting Standards Council) has conducted annual surveys of public attitudes towards taste and has tracked actual changes in broadcasting through a content analysis of programming since 1991. Using a panel of audience monitors who complete viewing diaries, the Commission's 'Audience Monitoring Studies' have found similar opinions about what results in offence to viewers and what type of programmes are sources of offence from violence as the ITC's studies. In 1999, half of the monitors said there were issues of concern to them on television. Of these, 39 per cent spontaneously mentioned violence as a source of concern, 25 per cent were concerned by swearing and offensive language, and 21 per cent were concerned about sex on television.[8] Although levels of concern are seen to fluctuate year to year, the position of violence as the most common cause for concern has remained unchanged for a decade Since the Commission's surveys began in 1991, most respondents have reported that there is 'too much' violence on television year after year although numbers are slowly declining. Whilst the majority of viewers still feel there is too much rather than 'too little' or 'about the right amount' of violence on television, the proportion who say there is too much has fallen from 67 per cent in 1991 to 59 per cent in 1999.[9] Of those who felt there was 'too much' violence in 1999, half said they had been offended by violence, whilst others said whether they would be offended or not would depend either on the programming context or whether children were in the audience. In 1997 monitors were asked to rate the amount of bad language, explicit sex or violence that they felt programmes contained. Of the average 37.5 they reported on, 5 per cent were rated between 3 and 5 on a scale of 1-5.[10] Monitors were also asked to report incidences of programmes that contained what they felt was unjustified violence. They found scenes of unjustified violence in 5.6 per cent and 6.8 per cent of films, 3.6 per cent and 2 per cent of drama/drama series, 0.5 per cent and <0.5 per cent in news/current affairs and 0.7 per cent and 1 per cent in documentaries in 1996 and 1997 respectively.[11]

Levels of offence resulting from televised violence therefore vary across genres that can be roughly divided between factual and fictional programmes. The following section explores in more depth some of the reasons why people are offended by violent content in factual programmes, and the following chapter considers audience perceptions of violence in factual genre.

News and current affairs

The 1993 Broadcasting Standards Council's *Annual Review of Violence in Factual Television* reported the findings of its survey into the viewers' relationship with factual programmes (Millwood Hargrave, 1993). The review consisted of a national representative survey of 1296 adults and a report from video edit groups undertaken at the Institute of Communications Studies, University of Leeds (Morrison and MacGregor, 1993, and for a more full account of the study see Morrison, 2000). The groups used an innovative new research method developed by the Institute in which groups of viewers were shown clips from factual programmes and allowed to edit them in line with their own opinions concerning what was and wasn't acceptable.[12] The research findings regarding News and Current Affairs will be presented in this section.

The national survey found that people felt a sense of duty to watch the news; that they felt they had an obligation to keep themselves informed about current events. Viewers were of the opinion that if a newsworthy event occurred, it should be reported no matter how violent it was (however, results from the edit groups demonstrate the visual limits placed on violence shown). Violence in the news was found to be more acceptable than in fictional programming because it was real, and because of the sense that viewers had a civic duty to keep themselves informed. This acceptance does not mean that viewers did not find factual violence upsetting (the edit groups showed this), in fact many said it was more upsetting than fictional violence because it was real. Indeed, it was the disturbing nature of some news that prompted people to say that children should be protected from the worst images via the Watershed and, in some cases, a warning should be given prior to broadcasting (these issues are to be discussed in later chapters).

Morrison and MacGregor's video editing group study was conducted in Spring 1993 and involved 10 groups of men and women, 7-8 in each, from socio-economic groups C1/C2. The groups were split into age categories of 16-24, 25-34, 40-55, 55+, and satellite viewers under 50. In the genre of News and Current Affairs the groups were shown three sequences: a British local news bulletin highlighting violence and its consequences in which a man had had his ear bitten off in a brawl outside a bar; news coverage of the Vietnam war showing several different scenes including a girl burnt by napalm running away, a woman cradling a burnt baby and a Vietcong suspect being shot at point blank range; and finally a report from the Bosnian war about atrocities allegedly committed by Muslims.

The local news item showed graphic shots of the victim's wound and was accompanied by a detailed commentary including a description of the fight in dramatically graphic terms. Each group voiced different criticisms of the report but most agreed it had over-sensationalised the event. It was clear that viewers did not want the news to dramatise events or create sensation. They regarded the news as the purest form of factual programme (25-34 males) and objected to the dramatic use of the voice over. Some of the women (16-24) pointed out that they did not need to know as many of the facts as a jury might in a criminal trial, and therefore objected to the level of detail provided by the programme. The older groups, particularly women, were more likely to be shocked by the level of violence reported. The shock value was removed for others, notably the 24-35 men, by the judgement that the men involved in the reported brawl were the 'type' of persons used to such violence. The evidence gathered suggested that the groups would have been more shocked and indeed more sympathetic if the victim was seen to be the type of person not used to being caught up in such violence such as a schoolteacher. The Vietnam footage was received differently to the above. Not only was it past news, but most of the groups had seen it at least once before. The scenes shocked all of the groups, particularly the shooting of the Vietcong suspect. One young man said, "to me the last 20 seconds of his life are more shocking than the act of being shot."[13] Women, particularly those who were mothers, tended to be more upset than the men by the pictures of the injured baby. The napalmed young girl received less sympathy as she was seen as more capable of looking after herself than a baby, and in addition had managed to escape the combat zone. Levels of sympathy and, by extension, emotional upset, as responses to the scene were dependent on the perceived and accorded status of the victim. The relationship between sympathy, subsequent upset, and the perceived status of the victim, was again demonstrated by the response of a female satellite viewer. She described how, as a mother, she had sympathy for the baby and found the scene very disturbing. With regard to the Vietcong man and the napalmed girl, she felt more strongly for the man because he had lost his life, whilst the girl had survived. However, her feelings for him weakened after she was told that the man was suspected of several murders, thus demonstrating how changing the status of the individual affects emotional response.

Despite the distress caused by the Vietnam footage most respondents felt that it was necessary and acceptable to show the pictures. One of the 55+ women said 'Although it was horrible, it was the news, it was factual, it was war.'[14] Most groups expressed a desire for the material to be shown after the Watershed, others suggested a less graphic pre-Watershed version, whilst some people proposed a warning. Interestingly, the 40-55 year old women pointed out that if the footage was from a current war there would be more justification in broadcasting it as news at any time, but since the material featured in a documentary it should be shown post Watershed. What appears to be operating, and is supported by the previously mentioned survey results, is the principle of 'need to know', or 'duty to be informed' about current events, a principle that did not apply so firmly to past events. Even so, the Bosnian footage shown to the groups clearly demonstrated that the 'need to know' principle has limits of acceptability.

The Bosnia material showed men digging up dead bodies, and clearly showed corpses laid out on the ground. The footage was accompanied by a voice over describing how the men had been tied up with barbed wire and their heads and hands had been cut off. More gruesome untransmitted footage was also shown to the groups. Several of the groups found the close ups of the dead bodies unacceptable. They thought that wide shots of the bodies would be more appropriate on the grounds that close ups of the exhumed bodies would not add further enlightenment to the report. Verbal descriptions were enough to explain the situation. As one man (16-24) pointed out, the state of decomposition of the bodies had more relevance to the length of time that they had been buried and was not relevant to the story about how the war was being conducted.

In contrast some groups, including men aged 24-34 and 40-55, approved of the inclusion of the imagery in order to verify the claims of the voice report, but did not agree that gruesome footage should be included simply to increase the impact of the report. They thought it important for people to see the truth with their own eyes. However, one man did confess that the geographical and cultural distance of the war lessened the impact of such imagery. He said he would have been far more disturbed by similar scenes from somewhere closer to home, such as Enniskillen, Northern Ireland the location of an IRA bomb attack in 1987. As with the Vietnam pictures, calls were made for edited pre-Watershed versions and warnings to be used, mainly to protect children. Again, women were more sensitive to the images of death than men. They tended to view the pictures in terms of tragedies rather than the unfolding events of war. In considering the suitability of the un-transmitted footage and other disturbing material, the groups brought attention to the differences between news and documentaries. It was thought that documentaries should elaborate on the basic information provided by the news. In terms of the shock effect of the pictures, one woman explained that it was in some ways easier to accept such pictures in documentaries because viewers were more likely to know beforehand the type of scenes that might be transmitted.

In 1998 a further video editing group study was commissioned as part of an initiative by the broadcasting industry to gain a fuller understanding of the way in which viewers define violence (Morrison, 2000 and for an edited version see Morrison, 1999). The research sought to explore viewers' definitions of screen violence in order to discover whether or not there are central features of violent acts that constitute a single definition of violence common to all viewers. In addition to this aim, the research encompassed the issues of the acceptability, enjoyment and justification of screen violence and the effect of genre on definitions of violence. The research used the original video editing method, but employed new digital technology to enable respondents to edit material at a faster pace and to a more sophisticated level than in the 1993 study.[15]

In addition to standard demographics and geographic location the members of the twelve edit groups were recruited according to various characteristics to maximise the possibility of diversity in their responses to violence. Groups were conducted with men and women familiar with real life violence (most usually street and pub violence), policemen, cable/satellite film subscribers, women with a fear of crime, men and women with children, and men and women over 60 (this group included some war veterans). The research concluded that there was a commonly held definition of violence, regardless of personal characteristics. This shared view of what constituted violence was held to be structured by a shared set of values about what is and is not appropriate behaviour. For the purposes of this review the following discussion of the study will focus on reporting the respondents' perceptions of the material used rather than the process of them arriving at a definition of violence. The conclusions of the research in terms of how viewers come to define violence are covered later as part of an examination of the participants' perceptions of the fictional material used in the study.

The groups were shown violence from a wide range of material, including Hollywood films, British drama, crime drama, news and war news. In the genre of news the respondents viewed three items:

(1) A Channel Four news report on the practice of bear baiting in Pakistan.

(2) Unedited rushes of an interview in which a tourist convicted for stealing a teddy bear from a pile of tributes left outside Kensington Palace after the death of Princess Diana was punched by a drunk.

(3) The news story compiled and transmitted from these rushes.

The bear baiting item featured bears chained to a stake and attacked by dogs in Pakistan. The story included close up shots of the bears prior to the fight showing that their teeth and claws had been removed. All of the groups condemned the practice as 'sick and unfair'. The fight was judged an unequal contest due to the inability of the bears to fully defend themselves. The fact that the fight had been organised purely for human entertainment intensified the distress felt by some of the respondents. Whilst it was considered permissible to show animals fighting in the wild, it was not considered correct to contrive cruelty to animals as a form of entertainment. Thus, the notion of the bears as innocent, defenceless victims, exploited and abused for entertainment, influenced viewers' perception of the report as violent. Having said that, despite the distressing scenes, viewers considered it right to include such material in a special news report because the clip was held to have an acceptable point and purpose – to expose the evils of bear baiting.

Each group was shown both the unedited rushes and the actual news item of an incident involving a drunk and a convicted tourist convicted of stealing a memento left to commemorate Princess Diana. In the rushes, the viewers saw an obviously drunk middle-aged man lurking behind the tourist who is being interviewed by reporters. The drunk, unsteady on his feet, appears behind the man and verbally abuses him several times, accusing him of 'mugging my Diana', before punching him on the side of the head in a drunken manner. Although the tourist is seen to be shocked, it is clear that he has not been badly injured. In contrast, the broadcast edited news story omits the build up to the attack, only showing the man approach the tourist and deliver the punch. Whilst none of the groups found either of the versions particularly violent, the majority of respondents agreed that the broadcast edited version was more violent than the rushes.

Morrison suggests that several factors contribute to the participants' definition of the rushes as more violent than the transmitted news report. It is obvious in the unedited footage that the assailant is extremely drunk and incapable of inflicting serious harm on the victim. The manner in which he stumbles around behind the tourist for some time, offering slurred abuse, allows the viewer time to predict the outcome. In the edited version the course of events is shortened, and the frame sharpened, with the result that the blow looks more vicious than in the rushes. Several respondents also noticed that the sound level in the news item had been increased to heighten the impact of the punch, which in turn amplified their perception of it as violent.

Several of the participants found the footage amusing despite the violent incident. Morrison suggests that the perception of the event as comical rather than violent resulted from a common lack of empathy with the victim. The foreign tourist spoke poor English and conducted the interview with a persistent smirk on his face. This performance aroused little sympathy amongst the respondents who felt that he 'got what he deserved' for stealing from the tributes. Thus, the groups did not find the material distressing or upsetting despite their definition of it as violent.

War News

Research shows that violence in war reports is perceived differently from violence that occurs in civilian circumstances. War is war and it is expected to be violent. For example, a study of audience opinions on television coverage of the 1991 Gulf war found similar attitudes amongst viewers to those expressed in relation to the Vietnam and Bosnian war footage mentioned earlier (Morrison, 1992). In a nationally representative survey viewers were asked to consider four events broadcast at the time of the war that each fuelled widespread debate on their morality and acceptability.

The reports covered:

(1) The bombing of the Amiriya bunker/shelter in Baghdad resulting in heavy civilian casualties.

(2) The coalition forces pilots captured by Iraq and displayed on Iraqi television.

(3) The filming of the Iraqi troops surrendering.

(4) The aftermath of the coalition attacks on Iraqi forces as they were withdrawing from Kuwait along the road to Basra in the final days of the conflict.

The majority of respondents (70 per cent) felt it was right to show all the footage on British television apart from that concerning the coalition pilots, which was opposed by 57 per cent.[16] The main justification for showing the other material was that the true effect of war should be shown by television news. Forty per cent of people also thought that it was only right to show that the pilots were still alive whilst others said that some footage should be broadcast simply to show the Iraqis in a bad light.[17] Various reasons were given for not showing certain footage. Many people believed that in the cases of reports 1 and 4 they could use their imagination to grasp the detail of what happened and did not need to see such graphic pictures. Others thought that some of the pictures were too upsetting to be shown. This opinion was voiced specifically with regard to the pilots where there was great concern for their relatives (the perceptions of survivors of violence and their relatives will be discussed later). There was also concern that scene 3 created sympathy for the Iraqi soldiers which might result in a lowering of support for the war effort among the British people

Focus groups were used to test responses to different levels of coverage of the bombing of the Amiriya bunker. The groups were shown reports of the bombing that had been transmitted at the time of the war by the BBC, ITN and WTN.[18] The BBC and ITN films used edited footage of the human devastation caused by the strike, whilst the WTN film used more explicit material showing charred bodies, which were so badly burnt that the human form was hardly recognisable. The BBC and ITN material was accepted by most of the groups despite its distressing nature because it was held to have a clear purpose and explained what had occurred without lingering on the detail of human injury. In contrast the WTN footage was deemed to go far beyond what was necessary to explain the event that had occurred. The function of the news was seen to be to report what was happening in terms of the events of the war, which included injuries, but this did not include graphic close up shots that went beyond establishing what had happened. As in other research (Morrison and MacGregor, 1993), the differences between such material being used for news as opposed to documentary purposes were highlighted. Respondents held that more graphic material could be shown in documentaries for the reasons already advanced; namely that the viewer would expect, and therefore be mentally prepared for, violent images in a documentary that was known to be about war.

Morrison's research also demonstrated how the audience discriminates between war and civilian news, and how sympathies are affected by the status of the victims. Respondents were asked, in the survey part of the research, to consider three imaginary scenarios for television reports in which coverage ranged from close up pictures of the dead and injured to purely verbal descriptions with no pictures of casualties. The scenarios were:

(1) A serious train crash.

(2) Land battles involving Iraqi casualties.

(3) Land battles involving British casualties.

Only 11 per cent of people agreed that close ups of the dead and injured would be acceptable in any of the scenarios. The amount of people who agreed that the scenes should only be filmed from a distance so that the dead could not be recognised were 47 per cent for the train crash, 48 per cent for the British soldiers, and 42 per cent for the Iraqi soldiers.[19] It was thought marginally more acceptable to show the faces of dead Iraqis than dead British. Again, more people agreed that the scene should only be shown after the dead and badly injured had been removed for the train crash (43 per cent)[20] than for the military scenes where 34 per cent thought that it was acceptable to only show the scene after the dead and badly injured had been removed in the case of British soldiers and 28 per cent in the case of Iraqi soldiers. A comparison of these results shows the increased sensitivity of the viewer when an event is not military and is close to home. Furthermore, it is noteworthy that personal identification with the dead (British soldiers as opposed to Iraqi soldiers) increases sensitivity. Morrison also suggests that there is more support for showing violent imagery of war than for civilian accidents because there is a justifiable purpose to showing the full horrors of war – such pictures act as a reminder that 'war has human consequences which politically we ought to confront'.[21]

Similar findings are reported in *Violence on Television: What the Viewers Think.* (1988) by Barrie Gunter and Mallory Wober. In a survey of public response to footage of the Falklands war they asked respondents whether all or only part of the material available should be shown. In the case of pictures of dying or wounded soldiers 18 per cent thought that all of the available footage should be shown of Argentine soldiers, but only 14 per cent thought the same for British soldiers,[22] 42 per cent were in favour of only showing part of the available material featuring British soldiers whereas slightly less 37 per cent thought the same about showing Argentine dead or wounded.[23] Thus, the respondents were not only saying that very few of them wanted to see all the available material but that they were only marginally less sensitive about seeing explicit coverage of dying or wounded Argentine soldiers. It is interesting, for example, that when Gunter and Wober asked about footage showing bereaved British and Argentine families the responses differed: slightly fewer respondents were in favour of not showing all of the available material concerning bereaved British families (38 per cent) than for footage showing bereaved Argentine families (40 per cent).[24] Respondents were therefore virtually equally keen to protect the feelings and privacy of bereaved British and Argentinean families, as both were seen as innocent. Gunter and Wober believe this demonstrates the viewer's concern that trauma and suffering should not be added to by invasion of privacy.[25]

Footage from war news was also shown to respondents in Morrison's study of viewers' definitions of violence (Morrison 1999, 2000). The following material was used:

(1) A report on the aftermath of the Sarajevo market place bombing broadcast by Sky news.

(2) A report using the same footage as the Sky report of the Sarajevo market place bombing but featuring the aftermath in greater graphic

detail, including a headless body being dragged that had been transmitted by Croatian Television (HRT).

(3) An unedited Reuters news feed of footage from Tuzla, Bosnia, showing the aftermath of a mortar bomb attack on a café. The feed showed, in graphic detail, bodies being loaded into a van, including a close up of a head almost detached from its body.

None of the groups defined any of the material as violent. Respondents found the footage unpleasant and defined the content as the aftermath of violence not violence as such. The groups were especially distressed by scenes from the Tuzla bombing, which featured very graphic pictures of human devastation the like of which the participants had never before witnessed. Several of the respondents mentioned that they found the footage more upsetting and shocking than any of the fictional violence they were shown as part of the study. As in the case of the bear baiting news item shown to groups, it was acknowledged that such footage had a point and purpose and thus should be shown to illustrate the tragedies of the war. Even so, it was generally felt that the same message could have been achieved without such graphic detail. Reiterating the views of respondents in Morrison's Gulf War study, the respondents felt that although it was important to understand what had happened, it was not necessary to see the exact nature of the injuries.

Documentaries

The concept of the use of violent imagery as more acceptable in documentaries than news reports was a common finding of much of the research reviewed (Millwood Hargrave, 1993; Morrison, 1992). Viewers believe that, as long as the Watershed is applied and warnings about disturbing material are given, then explicit material can be shown in documentaries, providing it is used to make a valid point. Gratuitous use of violence is not tolerated in any form and, as further discussion of Morrison and MacGregor's 1993[26] video edit groups will show, sensationalism and dramatisation is also not approved of.

The groups were shown material from three different documentaries: *Viewpoint '93* which investigated the psychological make up of serial killers and included an interview with the serial killer, Dennis Nilsen; an edition of *World in Action* which reported the case of a man who was held captive in his own flat and raped and tortured by two men; and an American 'fly on the wall' documentary called *Cops* which followed the work of the police and showed the violent arrest of a man.

One of the main complaints about *Viewpoint '93* was that it did not have a justifiable purpose. In the programme Nilsen spoke in graphic terms about the murders he had committed, describing how he had chopped the bodies up with a saw. Interestingly, viewers were more disturbed by the way Nilsen talked about the murders than by any of the imagery shown. Respondents said that they could not understand what purpose seeing the film would have to the public. The strongest of these views came from a male satellite viewer who said, 'The public had not been served anything from that, absolutely nothing wrong in producing that for experts, pathologists, if it's an insight into them sort of persons, but what the hell is me, or the public getting from that, I just don't know'.[27] This echoes a viewpoint highlighted by research into the news genre; viewers consider the showing of violent scenes justifiable only if the display of violence lends purpose and point to the story. Footage must have some intellectual or social relevance to the viewer. Another point raised by a member of the group of 40-55 year old men was that individuals such as Nilsen should not, on moral grounds, be given the opportunity to express themselves in public. This respondent was outraged that someone such as Nilsen should be given the opportunity to explain his or her actions. Another concern common to the groups was for the relatives of the victims. They thought that a programme containing such explicit descriptions of the violence inflicted on victims would be likely to cause extreme distress to any friends or family that might be watching. It is also worth noting that several viewers who had seen the original broadcast of the programme said that they had been disturbed by it to the extent that the memory of it had stayed with them for longer than any fictional violence they had ever seen.

The edition of *World in Action* shown to the groups featured a dramatic reconstruction of the kidnapping event described above. Stylistic techniques of slow motion, soft focus lenses and sound effects made the reconstruction more dramatic, especially in scenes showing a man being drowned in a bath and his body subsequently crashing through a glass window. All the groups thought that it was only suitable for transmission after the Watershed. Most of the groups also said that the use of dramatic techniques brought it closer to a drama than a documentary. They disagreed with the use of certain shots and elements of the sound track on the grounds that they over-sensationalised the story. One young man found the sound track particularly distasteful and others supported his view by saying that some of the scenes, such as the beating ought to have been described rather than visually depicted. Several groups, especially the 40-55 year old men and women, found the last two scenes which showed the victim being drowned in a bath of water and a body breaking through a glass door particularly distressing. Only after the breaking glass scene did the voice over clarify that the victim had not in reality been thrown through the glass but had jumped through it himself in order to escape. The older group of women was very upset by the fact that the film misled the viewer to believe that the victim had been drowned and that it was his dead body being thrown through the door. The fact that these women viewers did not fully understand what was going on, and were unaware that the victim was going to survive, added to their distress.

The research concluded that documentaries should not use dramatic effects to sensationalise violence and should avoid techniques that deliberately heighten suspense. In this particular documentary distress to viewers was increased owing to their sympathy for the victim who was characterised by the programme as vulnerable and innocent. The nature of the torture inflicted on the victim – rape and being bound by wire – was in itself sufficient to upset viewers. In particular, the women in the 25-34 age group found the use of the word 'rape' to have more violent and distressing connotations than the term 'sexual abuse'. Overall, of all the material shown, this clip was the most edited by all the groups and caused the most offence.

Cops featured the violent arrest of a young man, but viewers were not made aware of the reason for his arrest. The relationship between the perceived status of the victim and the viewers' reactions was clearly recognisable from the groups' reactions. Women in the 40-55 year old group were disturbed by the violence used in the arrest because as far as they knew he might not have done anything wrong. They therefore perceived the level of violence used to be unjustified and thus more shocking than if they had known he had committed a crime. The group of men aged 55+ found the level of violence intolerable for a different reason – they felt it was pointless. They did not consider that the programme had any educational or informative purpose and could not justify the violence on the sole grounds of its entertainment value.

Reconstruction Programmes

The editing groups were shown a reconstruction from the BBC programme *Crimewatch* in which actors were used to reconstruct a violent knife attack on a female shopkeeper. Viewers were also shown a black and white photograph of the facial injuries sustained by the actual victim accompanied by a voice over to explain what happened. In general the level of violent imagery used was seen as justified by the viewers on the grounds that *Crimewatch* was considered to be of public service by helping to apprehend criminals. In defence of the programme viewers also noted that the violence could be easily recognised as a reconstruction. Apart from the obviously bad/simplistic acting all noted that the use of a voice over helped to make it clear that the violence shown was reconstructed violence. This reduced the impact of what otherwise might have been a very disturbing scene indeed. Furthermore, the fact that the victim was shown to have made a full recovery further helped to reduce any distress caused. However, it is worth noting that both groups of older women said that the violence had an impact on them because of its setting in everyday reality and that due to their age, and hence relative frailty, they were sensitive to the fact that they themselves could easily fall victim to crimes of violence. Many of these women lived alone as a result of their partners having died, and confessed that watching such programmes on their own increased the impact of the violent imagery, and caused them to worry about the possibility of becoming victims of violence themselves. Their concerns were heightened because they had no one to discuss the programmes with and, so to speak, 'talk through' their fears with (fear of crime is discussed in more detail later).

Conclusions

Millwood Hargrave (1993) and Morrison & MacGregor (1993) make some conclusions from their studies of the audience's perceptions of different factual genres that are also evident in the research by Gunter & Wober (1988), Morrison (1992) and Morrison (2000). They suggest that four main factors that influence viewers' perceptions and reactions of violence in factual television are evident:

(1) *The Factor of Closeness* – The more distance, in terms of geography, time and other relationships, between the violence and the viewer, the less disturbing viewers will find it. For instance, building upon the qualitative work of Morrison and MacGregor, Millwood Hargrave's survey used the principles as guidelines and found that 82 per cent of people said they would be more upset by violence that involved people they could identify with.[28]

(2) *The Factor of Certainty* – Viewers are less likely to be shocked if they either know the outcome of a violent scene or if they fully understand what is happening in it.

(3) *The Factor of Status* – Viewers are likely to tolerate a higher degree of violence if the victim is regarded to have a lower claim to justice. Therefore a victim's perceived innocence is an important factor in how much violence will be accepted and how disturbing that violence is likely to be.

(4) *The Factor of Minimalism* – Violent imagery in factual programmes, whether it be real or reconstructed, should not use greater detail than is needed to illustrate the point being made. Furthermore, it should be noted that dramatic techniques such as sound tracks, slow motion and soft focus lenses could add to the distress caused to the viewer because such techniques heighten their engagement in the violence of the action. Morrison and MacGregor (1993) note that violence does not have to be graphic to be found disturbing and it is often the combination of images and wording that is distressing to viewers.

Some further observations can be drawn from the research reviewed.

Women, especially those who are mothers, are often distressed by violent imagery in which children are victims. They also tend to get more upset if their level of sympathy for the victim is high: this is usually directly related to the perceived innocence of the victim. Furthermore, women are made anxious by some violence, particularly if they can relate to it, by being able to imagine themselves as the victims.

Older people, particularly women and those who live alone, may be more sensitive to violence than others due to their fear of crime. This fear is a result of their increasing lack of ability to defend themselves due to infirmity and, if they live alone, the absence of anyone to help allay their fears through the discussion of violence in programmes.

Most viewers are more acceptant of violent imagery if the rules of the Watershed have been adhered to, or if viewers have been given warnings.

Viewers award each genre within factual programming different discretionary levels of violence; for example war news is perceived in a different light to domestic news.

Notes

1 Formerly known as *Attitudes to Television*. A comprehensive summary of the findings of the surveys, commissioned annually since 1970, can be found in Svennevig, M (1998).

2 Independent Television Commission (2001), p.34.

3 After 1993 respondents were not asked what particular aspects of particular types of programmes offended them, and after 1995 viewers were no longer asked which type of programmes caused them most offence - respondents are now asked about sources of offence in terms of channels.

4 Gunter, B & Winstone, P (1993) and Gunter, B, Sancho-Aldridge, J & Winstone, P (1994).

5 ibid.

6 Independent Television Commission (1995).

7 Gunter, B, Sancho-Aldridge, J & Winstone, P (op.cit.).

8 Broadcasting Standards Commission (2000) *Briefing update No6: Matters of Offence.*

9 ibid.

10 Broadcasting Standards Commission (1998) *Monitoring Report 6:1997.*

11 Broadcasting Standards Commission (1997) *Monitoring Report 5:1996* and Broadcasting Standards Commission (1998) *Monitoring Report 6:1997.* This line of questioning has not been pursued in subsequent years.

12 For a report on the video edit group method see Morrison, D.E & MacGregor, B (1995), and also for an explanation and substantive findings from the method see Morrison, D.E (2000) Chapter 6.

13 Morrison, D.E & MacGregor, B, (1993) p.70.

14 Op.cit p.72.

15 For a report on the original video edit group method see Morrison, D.E & MacGregor, B (1995), and also for an explanation and substantive findings from the method see Morrison, D.E (2000) Chapter 6.

16 Morrison, D.E (1992).

17 ibid.

18 WTN (Worldwide Television News) merged with Associated Press TV News in 1998.

19 Morrison, D.E (1992) p.32.

20 Op.cit, p.32.

21 Op.cit. p.34.

22 Gunter, B and Wober, M (1988).

23 ibid.

24 ibid.

25 See Morrison, D.E and Svennevig, M (2002) for a detailed study of when it is justifiable to intrude on privacy, including some responses to coverage of the events of September 11th 2001. See also Kieran, M, Morrison, D.E and Svennevig, M (2000) for the 'status rules' which influence the audience's interpretation of rights to privacy.

26 For a detailed description of the focus groups see Morrison, D.E (2000) Chapter 6.

27 Morrison, D.E and MacGregor, B, (1993) p.47. Also see Morrison, D.E (2000) Chapter 6.

28 Op.cit. p.18. See also Morrison, D.E (2000) Chapter 6.

2
Perceptions of violence in fictional television

The audience views factual violence in different terms to violence in fiction. For example, a viewer interviewed as part of Morrison and MacGregor's research into violence in factual television said of fictional violence: '... no matter how realistically any kind of acting is done, you always know it's fiction, there is always something that tells you that it's fictional and it acts as a kind of barrier.'[1] Overall, research has concluded that audiences find factual violence more upsetting than fictional violence. Nevertheless, viewers can and do find some instances of fictional violence a source of distress, and there is a substantial amount of research that explores the attitudes of the audience to such violence. Much of the research in this area demonstrates that matters of context determine the audience's perceptions of violence in fictional television.

Measuring violence

The most common method used to measure the salience of violence on television is that of content analysis.[2] Most content analyses use objective classifications of what types of acts are classified as violent that fail to take into account the complex and subjective way in which viewers define what constitutes a violent act. Barrie Gunter states, 'Television viewers, young and old, are selectively perceptive and judgmental in their responses to programmes. The ways viewers perceive and evaluate characters and events on television do not always match descriptive incident counts or the meanings inferred from them by researchers.'[3] Most content analyses of violence on television follow a basic coding system to record how many and what sort of violent acts occur in a programme, but in doing so pay little regard to matters of context. In contrast, viewers place violence in the context of the totality of a programme rather than as distinct incidents. As the review of research into perceptions of violence in factual television has already shown, viewers' perceptions of the meaning of violence always include an interpretative act. For instance, cartoons such as *Tom and Jerry* contain a significant amount of violent acts and would be classified as violent in content analysis studies, but are not necessarily seen as violent by viewers because of the fantastical and animated context in which the violence occurs. Therefore, the way the audience perceives violent acts in television programmes requires a more elaborate style of interpretation than that found in most content analyses of screen violence. In recognition of this limitation of the method, the annual content analysis of programming conducted by the Broadcasting Standards Commission in 1997 and 1998 for the first time used additional measures of context. The analysis included measures of fairness and justice, and divided incidents of violence into three categories; intentional/interpersonal violence, accidental violence, and aggression. More meaningful analyses such as this come closer to measuring the level of violence on television in a way that corresponds with audience perceptions of the amount of violence on television. The following studies demonstrate the complexity and range of factors employed in viewers' perceptions of fictional violence.

Matters of context

A research consortium of four American universities studied violence in the media between 1994 and 1997 for the 'National Television Violence Study' (1996, 1997, 1998). As part of the research they explored how the manipulation of contextual features in violent television portrayals influences the audience's reactions to violence.[4] Although the results of the study are taken from research using content analysis and in the area of effects, the findings make a pertinent contribution to understanding how audiences interpret and perceive violent imagery. The study found that, depending on how it is presented in a programme, violence can vary in its meanings to the viewer and produce differing reactions in terms of personal aggression, fear and desensitisation. The contextual factors that influence these meanings are broken down into categories by the study:

The Nature of the Perpetrator – violence carried out by a 'good guy' evokes different reactions than if a 'bad guy' is responsible.

The Nature of the Target – if the viewer is able to share the character's emotional experiences and perceives the character to be likeable, the level of fear felt by the viewer is increased.

The Presence of Weapons – guns are seen as the most violent weapons.

The Reason for Violence – unjustified violence is more likely to induce feelings of unease than socially sanctioned or altruistic violence. Therefore, violence used in self defence is seen as justified in a programme because the perpetrator of the violence is perceived as innocent and the victim is seen as guilty.

The Extent and Graphicness of Violence – the research reported that persistent close up camera shots of rough violence are interpreted by viewers as more violent than distance shots. It is also suggested that the more violence that is seen on television the more vulnerable the viewer feels due to an increased fear of crime.

The Realism of Violence – the more realistic the nature of the violence the more likely it is that viewers will be distressed. The example of *Star Wars* and *Silence of the Lambs* is given. The latter film was found to disturb viewers more than the former.

Rewards and Punishments – viewers' fears will be reduced if the perpetrator of the violence is seen to receive the punishment he/she deserves.

Consequences of Violence – the research drew upon the work of Barrie Gunter (1983, 1985) to suggest that the audience judges scenes in which violence results in observable harm and pain to be more violent than scenes that do not show the results of violence. This suggests that viewers' interpretations of fictional violence are based on a complex set of values and judgements about the various different elements that make up any violent act.

Genre

Barrie Gunter's study (1985) is illustrative of the complexities of the factors involved in responses to and perceptions of violence. His research involved twelve experimental studies in which subjects were shown clips from various fictional genres and asked how they felt about the violence portrayed in each. The programmes were as follows:

British Crime Series – *The Professionals* and *The Sweeney*.

American Crime Series – *Kojak*, *Starsky and Hutch* and *Mannix*.

Westerns – *Alias Smith and Jones* and *Cannon of Cordoba*.

Science Fiction – *Buck Rogers* and *Star Trek*.

Cartoons – *Mickey Mouse*.

Gunter made several judgements, based on viewers' reactions, that are reflected in some of the conclusions of the 'National Television Violence' study in the USA. He observed that the British respondents rated violent acts in British crime series as more violent than the violence in American crime drama series. He goes on to suggest that viewers' responses to fictional violence are affected in the same way as their responses to factual violence (see previous chapter); the closeness to home of violence has a profound effect. Violent behaviour in both the Cartoon and Science Fiction programmes was not classed as violent by the respondents because it was not seen to be seated in reality. Other factors such as the type of fictional characters who inflict the violence, how the harm is inflicted and how much damage is done to the recipient also have a bearing on how people view violence. Gunter's research also showed that the audience have clear opinions relating to the appropriateness of the strength and level of violence used. The subjects were concerned, and were more likely to be distressed, by violence used in acts of retaliation that did not seem appropriate to the act of provocation. One conclusion regarding crime genres is that the level of violence used to enforce the law should be appropriate to the crime committed – for instance, the shooting of a non-violent unarmed car thief by a policeman would be seen as an inappropriate response.

The effect of contextual factors is also discussed in *Violence in Television Fiction* by David Docherty(1990). Docherty conducted a survey that aimed to explore viewers' opinions on the suitability of violence in various contexts. Respondents were sent video tapes of three fictional programmes featuring violence and were asked, via a questionnaire, whether they would edit the programme before transmission and if so, how. The research examined the responses of the 79 viewers out of the original 250 contacted who returned the questionnaire.

Respondents were widely acceptant of the level of violence shown in the edition of the British crime drama serial *The Bill* that they watched. It depicted the killing by police marksmen of some bank robbers who had held a gun to a cashier's head. Three out of the 79 respondents wanted to edit the programme whilst the same number did not want it shown at all, but the majority of people were not upset or offended by the violence in the programme.[5]

The second programme was a BBC 2 drama about football hooliganism called *The Firm*. The drama featured several violent scenes including a young black boy having his face slashed, an infant putting a Stanley knife blade in his mouth and various violent gang fights. Some respondents were so disgusted by the violence that they refused to watch the programme and sent back the videotapes. Out of the 54 respondents aged 35 or over, 57 per cent did not want the drama to be transmitted whilst a significant number, 26 per cent, thought that it could be shown in its entirety.[6] Fewer of the viewers under 35 (33 per cent) did not want the drama to be broadcast and 50 per cent of this group had no problem with showing the drama in full. The main concern of those who did not want to see *The Firm* transmitted was that it glorified a certain type of violence, which they considered would encourage people to act in an irresponsible manner. One woman (over 35) said, 'I disliked everything about it. I think it encourages everything we want stamped out in this country and it helps to glorify mindless violence to those inclined.'[7] However, those who were in support of showing the drama in full thought that the violent imagery was necessary to effectively convey the programme's central message.

The third programme the respondents watched was the film, *Nightmare On Elm Street*. In this gory horror film a male character appears in people's dreams and inflicts various horrors upon them with scissor-like fingernails. It also includes particularly bloody special effects, which bring the film close to parody. The majority of people over 35 (60 per cent) thought the film could be transmitted in its entirety provided it was shown after the Watershed, and a similar proportion of the younger respondents (67 per cent) also thought it could be shown without editing. These respondents said they enjoyed the suspense of the film to the point of finding it amusing: 'because it was so over the top it was almost funny. The suspense was good and the idea that dreams could be real was intriguing' (Female under 35).[8] However, 25 per cent of the older respondents and 21 per cent of the younger ones did not think the film was suitable for transmission. They were disgusted by the violence, especially the bloody special effects which made some of them feel physically ill: "Too much violence, too far fetched, too bloody. It made me ill. I could not watch most of it. I hated the whole thing" (Female over 35).[9] Those respondents who thought the film could be broadcast, but only after editing, wanted to change the killing scenes, particularly the first gruesome murder.

Docherty applies the theory of deep and shallow play, originally developed by the anthropologist Clifford Geertz,[10] to his analysis of respondents' reactions to the violence in the programmes. From this he makes a generalised observation about the audience and suggests that viewers interpret violent imagery in different ways according to whether the context of the violence shown is based in deep or shallow play. He describes violence in deep-play fiction as that which viewers can directly relate to; for example, violence that is perceived to be indicative of British life. Docherty goes on to say that such fictional violence 'may trigger anxious concern about the possible effects of the images or resentment at the inaccurate depiction of British society'.[11] In contrast, violence in shallow-play fiction does not worry viewers because the violence featured is inflicted on a society that they cannot identify with, and therefore culturally and socially nothing is at stake. Docherty interprets the respondents' reactions to the above programmes in these terms. He explains that although *Nightmare on Elm Street* features violent actions which are significantly more bloody, it does not address deep-play issues such as those covered by *The Firm*. *Nightmare on Elm Street* is a horror film and as such the violence shown is socially, politically, and in the most part psychologically, removed from society. Subsequently viewers were distressed more by the squeamishness of the violence in the film than by the violent acts themselves. However, *The Firm* depicted violence rooted deep in the base of British society and for that reason evoked stronger, deep-play reactions from the respondents. Docherty does not use the theory to explain the respondents' responses to *The Bill*.

Characteristics of the viewer

In their research Barrie Gunter and Adrian Furnham (1984) take into account the effect that the particular psychological characteristics of a viewer may have on the way violence is perceived. Findings from behavioural effects research by Parke *et al.* (1977) prompted Gunter and Furnham to take the personal aggression levels of respondents into account when considering viewers' reactions to violent imagery. Parke and his colleagues suggested that 'enhancement of anti-social behaviours following exposure to a heavy diet of violent programming may be much more pronounced among individuals who are already aggressive than amongst non-aggressive types.'[12] Taking this as a starting point for analysing the perceptions of the respondents to violence,

Gunter and Furnham classified the personal aggressiveness levels of respondents in terms of whether they sought to resolve hypothetical situations through verbal or physical aggression. They found that respondents who tended towards verbal aggression perceived the violence shown in British Crime Dramas as more violent and disturbing than those who did not tend towards verbal aggression. Indeed, those who did not tend towards verbal aggression rated the same violence as less disturbing, less realistic and more humorous than their less aggressive counterparts.

As part of his research into viewers' definitions of violence, Morrison (2000) took the influence of personal characteristics and life experiences into account. As described earlier, individuals were recruited to take part in video edit groups from a variety of backgrounds. These included men and women familiar with real life violence, policemen, cable/satellite film subscribers, women with a fear of crime, men and women with children, and men and women over 60. Whilst the research did not find any major differences in definitions of violence to exist between the above groups, personal characteristics and life experiences were found to be a differentiating influence in issues of taste and decency. The study concluded that there is a commonly held definition of violence structured by a set of shared values about what is and is not appropriate behaviour. This is described in more detail below.

Forms of violence

Overall, research has found that some forms of physical violence are perceived to be more violent than others. In the National Television Study (1994-1997) shootings were found to be classed as more violent acts than stabbings, but were not found to be as disturbing, whilst fist fighting was the least distressing form of violent action. Research by the Broadcasting Standards Commission described in its 1997 Monitoring Report details what percentage of respondents would consider various acts to be violent if shown on TV. A knife attack was seen as the most violent act (85 per cent) whilst 56 per cent considered a gunfight violent and 53 per cent classed a fistfight as violent.[13] Gunter and Furnham (1984) suggest that one reason why viewers are more worried by stabbings than shootings might be the close contact nature of the violence. This does not, however, help to explain why fistfights are not seen as particularly violent since such violence is of a close contact nature. One can only assume that it is the serious nature of wounds inflicted by stabbings compared to injuries from fist blows that concern viewers. Furthermore, Gunter and Furnham propose that because stabbings are rarer than shootings in British crime drama, viewers may be more shocked by stabbings because they have become accustomed to, and thus desensitised to shootings. Gunter (1985) also found that, in general, viewers are more troubled by violence against women by men than vice versa. Such violence is especially distressing if it is featured in a scenario to which the viewer can readily relate. Figures in the Broadcasting Standards Commission report (1997) suggest that this may also be due to the unequal relationship between men and women in violent situations. Viewers consider any situation depicting an unequal contest as more violent than one where the perpetrators are considered equal. For example, a higher percentage of respondents considered the following three acts as more violent than a gun or fistfight (see above): an owner hitting his or her pet (73 per cent), a child being bullied by classmates (69 per cent), and a man verbally taunting a woman (60 per cent).[14] This demonstrates that viewers consider acts involving people of unequal standing as more violent than acts where the people involved are on an equal footing in terms of physical strength and ability to retaliate. However, Gunter (1985) also suggests that in some cases violence can be more disturbing if the perpetrator is a woman because viewers are used to seeing men as the main perpetrators of violence.

Morrison's (2000) study examined the influence of different forms of violence as well as other matters of context on viewers' definitions of violence. Morrison suggests that two factors are at work in a viewer's definition of an act as violent – these are referred to as primary and secondary definers. Primary definers of screen violence are drawn from real life definitions of violence. If an act is viewed as violent in real life then its screen portrayal will also be defined as violent. The basic underlying principle of this definition is that of fairness. Morrison suggests that the fairness of a situation is judged on the basis of several determinants: the distribution of power between the concerned parties including the status of the victim, and whether the violence is seen to be just and in proportion. Once a value judgement concerning the nature of the violence has been made using these primary definers, Morrison suggests that secondary definers are used to establish the degree of violence. Secondary definers concern specific contextual features of a violent act and are used to grade the level and impact of the violence. The most important contextual factor is the degree of realism presented by the portrayal. The degree of realism perceived by viewers is constructed from several contextual factors including the type of weapon used, sound effects, language, camera angles, and other dramatic effects. Therefore, 'the agreement as to whether or not something is violent is drawn from definitions of what constitutes violence in real life. However, how the actual level of violence is defined comes not from real life, but from learning how to define violence from watching violence on the screen.'[15]

The research demonstrates the role of primary and secondary definers in viewers' perceptions of violence by considering the reactions of the respondents to fictional violence shown to them. The groups were shown the following clips:

(1) *Thieftakers* – a British police television drama. Russian gangsters armed with machine guns ambush a meeting being held in a restaurant by British gangsters. The Russian leader unexpectedly headbutts his rival. Armed policemen arrive and a 'shoot out' ensues. Filmed in slow motion with a loud sound track, this action takes place in a shower of breaking glass and at one point depicts blood spurting from the back of a gangster as he is machine gunned.

(2) *Deep Cover*: a Hollywood crime/action film – A criminal who has spoken to the police is attacked with a pool cue in front of associates. Six graphic blows to the head and body are depicted, four of them in close up, and blood is seen spurting from his mouth.

(3) *Brookside*: a British soap opera. A man attacks his wife after the police call to investigate a neighbour's reports of domestic violence. No physical contact is shown because the attack takes place behind a sofa.

(4) *Ladybird, Ladybird* – A British realist drama film made for television. A violent attack by a man on his wife in front of their small children. He hits her with his fist, kicks her and smashes a beer can on the floor just missing her face. Violent, abusive language is used throughout including the 'c' word.

The participants described the gun fight in *Thieftakers* as violent. However, they did not take the violence seriously considering it to be unrealistic. It was recognised by the groups that the event had been dramatised to 'up the pace' of the storyline and several unrealistic aspects of the clip were identified. For example, it was considered an inaccurate portrayal of police activity because the police were not suitably equipped for the conflict with body armour and automatic weapons. The depiction of the injuries sustained from machine guns was thought 'over the top'. Whilst a dramatic slow motion shot of a bullet passing through a body was felt to increase the impact of the violence, it was also held to contribute to the unbelievable manner of the scene. One woman commented that although the close up increased the impact of the violence, it still was not realistic enough to make her feel squeamish. All the groups considered the headbutt the most violent part of the scene. Morrison suggests that the reason for this is that injuries inflicted through close physical contact are more distressing to viewers than other violence. Whilst gunfire could be predicted from the beginning of the scene, the headbutt was unexpected and increased the level of the violence through its shock value. In the specific case of the women who had been recruited specifically because they were fearful of becoming a victim of crime, Morrison observed that these women viewed and discussed all of the material in more emotional terms than the other groups. They were especially concerned by violent situations which they could envisage happening to themselves. Therefore, they found the headbutt more distressing than the gunshots because they considered that 'anybody can headbutt, but not many people have guns'.[16] Thus, the groups defined *Thieftakers* as violent, but were not distressed or concerned by the violence featured because of its unrealistic nature.

All the groups considered that the violence in *Deep Cover* was stronger than the violence in the *Thieftakers* clip. The differences in these estimations can be explained by reference to Morrison's concept of primary and secondary definers of violence. The status of the victim is unclear and therefore the appropriateness of the punishment questionable. Sympathy for the victim is further contributed to by his inability to fight back. The distribution of power between the assailant and the victim is unfair – in the words of one of the participants 'it is not a fair fight'. Whilst primary definers of violence were in place to effect the judgement that the scene was violent, the presence of secondary definers increased the violence of the scene.

The most important element in forming the groups' perception of the scene as violent was its realism. For example, many of the participants considered that the sound of the impacts during the beating, the victim's screams and begs for mercy, and the use of bad language made the scene seem authentic and, consequently, violent. Indeed, when some of the groups edited these sounds out using the previously mentioned video editing technique, they concluded that the scene was less violent. Physical elements of the beating, such as blood spurting from the victim's mouth, also contributed to the participants' perception of the portrayal as accurate, again heightening the level of perceived violence. This shared perception of the portrayal as realistic meant that the definition of the scene as violent was universal. However, the scene was not universally enjoyed. The young men and women with an experience of violence said they enjoyed it and found that type of screen violence entertaining, but the older men and women failed to find such violence enjoyable.

Viewers in the study felt that the violence in *Deep Cover* was realistic, but they considered the domestic violence in *Brookside* and *Ladybird, Ladybird* even more realistic. Morrison suggests that this is because the violence in *Deep Cover* was of a type that was far removed from the lives of the viewers. In contrast, the groups could relate more readily to the issue of domestic violence and were aware of its presence in society. It was, as Morrison terms it, 'authentic violence'. The participants described the clips as 'sad' and 'awful' as well as violent. Nevertheless, they considered, as with violence in news programmes, that programmes about domestic violence had an important point and purpose to convey, and therefore, the violent portrayals of domestic violence were justifiable.

Primary and secondary definers structured the groups' perceptions of the level of violence in the two dramas. Although very little actual violence was shown in *Brookside*, the unfair relationship between the husband and wife, the innocence of the victim and the implication of violence contributed to the participants' classification of the scene as violent. Many of them commented on the role of sound – the impact of the punches was heard but not seen – in making the scene violent. The groups described *Ladybird, Ladybird* as much more violent than *Brookside*. The material depicted a similar situation, but the impact of the violence was increased through contextual factors that emphasised the brutality of the scene. Not only was the husband shown kicking and punching the wife at the same time as verbally abusing her, but he returns and continues the beating after it appears to be over. The participants considered that, although language itself could not be defined as violence, it did add to the violence of the scene, especially the use of the 'c' word. As already mentioned, the groups viewed both scenes of domestic violence with more emotion than any of the other violence shown. The emotive impact of

Ladybird, Ladybird was amplified for the participants by the inclusion of a shot of children witnessing the attack. Whilst the groups concluded that their presence did not make the scene more violent, it was felt that the exposure of the children to the attack included them as victims of the violence. Morrison suggests that their inclusion in the scene represents not only an assault on the social ideal of the relationship between husband and wife, but also the destruction of a family.

The research concluded that the clip from *Ladybird, Ladybird* contained practically all the components considered by viewers to constitute violence. It is described as an example of violence in its purest form because it involved a helpless victim, fear, repetitive blows, injury continuing long past establishing a point, unequal distribution of power, violence out of proportion to the offence committed, and language as assault. Based on these primary definers of violence the scene was indeed defined as violent by all the groups. The perception of the portrayal as realistic, and the participants' ability to place the violence featured within the parameters of their own lives meant that they defined it as very violent. In fact the violence was considered so 'authentic' that some of the participants likened it to a documentary.

Based on the findings of the research, Morrison suggests that screen violence can be categorised into three main types:

Playful violence – This is violence that is clearly acted and is described as: not related to direct personal experience/expectations, surreal or unreal, not meant to be taken seriously, choreographed not to be taken as real, stereotyped rather than in depth.

Depicted violence – This is violence that is characterised by realism and is described as: detailed portrayal of violent acts, choreography to be taken as real, not related to direct personal experience, happy or just desert rather than sad or unjust.

Authentic violence – This is violence that takes place in a world that the viewer can recognise and is described as: known personal world either physically or psychologically, detailed portrayal of violent acts, choreographed to be unmistakably real, direct link to personal experience, unpredictable twists, endings.

From the findings of the study, Morrison constructed a general definition of violence: 'Screen violence is any act that is seen or unequivocally signalled so that viewers feel that they have seen an act which would be considered an act of violence in real life, which in effect means that the violence was considered unjustified either in the degree or nature of the force used, or that the injured party was undeserving of the violence. The degree of violence is defined by how realistic the violence is considered to be, and made even stronger if the violence inflicted is considered unfair.'[17]

Conclusions

Based on the above studies it is clear that perceptions of violence in fictional television are determined by a complex combination of factors. These include the context within which the violence occurs and the genre in which it is featured. It is also suggested that perceptions of violence, at least in some of the studies, are influenced by the viewer's own experiences and disposition. Whether violence will upset or disturb viewers will be largely determined by the following considerations:

Realistic Violence

Gunter (1985) found that violence in Cartoons and Science Fiction did not particularly bother viewers because it was not regarded as real violence. Docherty's (1990) study showed that the use of fantastical special effects in *Nightmare on Elm Street* resulted in respondents viewing the film as far fetched and most importantly, in the light of Gunter's findings, unrealistic. The majority of respondents were not concerned by the violence in the film.

Docherty's theory of deep and shallow play draws its importance in terms of media analysis from the way in which it treats symbolic portrayals as drawing their meanings from variations in reality. Elements of deep-play violence are determined by whether they seem realistic to the viewer. Violence in Cartoons, Science Fiction, Westerns and Horror movies can be seen as shallow play, and as such has less power to upset viewers than deep play. Morrison's study (2000) also notes the importance of viewers' perceptions of violence as realistic in defining an act as violent. The research shows that viewers are most likely to be distressed by violence defined as real and that which can be located within everyday life.

Identification with violence

The nature of violence and the way it is defined and incorporated into the viewer's mental world is determined by whether viewers can relate to it or not, and how the viewer places the violence in terms of their own experiences and understandings of violence. Gunter (1985) observed that violence that was geographically closer to home was rated as more violent by the audience than that which was distant. Docherty's (1990) theory of deep and shallow play states that violence that does not put anything at stake, culturally or socially, is not distressing to the viewer; this suggests that if violence does not disturb viewers' own concept of reality, they will not be concerned. Morrison (2000) describes violence with which the viewer can easily identify with as 'authentic violence', and suggests that this type of violence has the ability to strongly assault viewers' sensibilities.

Status of the Victim

Both the National Television Violence Study (1996,1997,1998) and Morrison's research (2000) found that viewers were more disturbed by violent acts towards a person whom they perceive as innocent than to someone whom they see as guilty, and deserving of punishment. Furthermore, Morrison suggests that the fairness of the power relationship between the victim and the perpetrator influences the audiences' perception of the level of the violence. Viewers' empathy with the victim is important in judging a situation as violent. Similar findings were seen in studies of viewers' perceptions of violence in factual programmes.

Forms of Violence

Gunter and Furnham (1984) suggest that the audience rate some forms of violence as more violent than others with guns/shootings seen as the most violent forms of behaviour. It should also be noted however, that viewers can be equally distressed by scenarios in which violence involves close contact even if guns are not used. Violence shot 'up close' is more disturbing than scenes shot from a distance. Gunter (1985) shows that the audience is more upset by scenes where the harm and pain inflicted by the violence is observable. Morrison (2000) observed that violence that continues for longer than is thought appropriate is disturbing to viewers. The study also showed that soundtracks can contribute to a viewer's perception of a scene as violent.

Whether the audience perceives a scene as violent, and thus potentially disturbing or distressing, is not determined by any one single contextual factor, but by a complex combination of many. The complicated role of context is epitomised in viewers' perceptions, and subsequent reaction to the violence in *Nightmare on Elm Street* shown to viewers in Docherty's study(1990). Much of the violence in the film is unjustified and inappropriate, the victims are innocent, the perpetrator is a 'bad guy', and much of the violence is of a graphic nature, yet only a minority of the respondents did not find the violence acceptable or were disturbed by it. The explanation for this lies in the unrealistic context of the violence and underscores many of the points drawn from the other research reviewed. In particular, in order to understand the emotional impact of screen violence one must first understand the perceptions individuals have of violence and the meanings that they attribute to it.

Notes

1 Morrison, D.E and MacGregor, B, (1993) p.11. Also see Morrison, D.E (2000) Chapter 6.
2 For a review of content analyses see Potter, W.J. (1999).
3 Gunter, B (1988).
4 For a fuller description of the studies see Chapter 6: 'Research In Other Countries' – USA.
5 Docherty, D (1990) p.28.
6 Op.cit. p.28.
7 Op.cit. p.29.
8 Op.cit. p.30.
9 Op.cit. p.30.
10 Geertz, Clifford (1993).
11 Docherty, D (1990) p.9.
12 Parke *et al.* (1997).
13 BSC Monitoring Report 5 (1997) p.72.
14 BSC Monitoring Report 5 (1997). p.72.
15 Morrison, D.E. (2000) p.451.
16 Op.cit. p.533.
17 Op.cit. p.453.

3
Children's Perceptions of Violence on Television
Cause for Concern

The overwhelming body of research examining for effects of the media on behaviour has concentrated on children and their propensity for imitative aggressive responses to that which they watch, read or hear.[1] Undoubtedly a general concern exists about the effect that watching violent programmes might have on children. Yet it is significant that in the course of his research into children's responses to violence on television, David Buckingham (1996)[2] found that concern amongst parents that children may become violent as an effect of watching violence was almost always voiced with reference to 'other people's' children. Parents' fears about the possible negative impacts of violence on television for their own children pertained to their children becoming frightened or traumatised by violence in either fictional or factual television, but not to the likely imitative influence television may have on their own children. As we will see from the research reviewed in this chapter, this view is realistic.

In a research paper produced in 1996 for the Broadcasting Standards Council James Halloran and Peggy Gray examined young people's attitudes to the media and the views of parents concerning the effect of television on people. They noted that the dominant view held by parents was that there is too much violence on television.[3] Their research also showed, in line with Buckingham's findings, that parents did not believe that such violence adversely affected *their* children, although they did consider that 'other people's' children might copy violence that they saw on television. For instance, the mother of a 14 year old girl said, '*The Bill* is influential, it tells you how to do things',[4] and the father of a 14 year-old boy said 'I don't like it (meaning violence on television), but it won't harm him because he is well balanced.'[5] When asked in what areas of programming they restricted their children's viewing, parents predominantly mentioned those programmes that contained sex rather than violence. When parents said that they wished to restrict the amount of violence that their children viewed on television, the reason for doing so was usually that they were worried that children might be frightened by what they saw, rather than because they thought children might be encouraged to behave violently. In their study *Young People New Media* (1999) Sonia Livingstone and Moira Bovill asked parents about a range of possible negative effects they believed television could have on their children. In the survey of 950 parents, 32 per cent agreed their child was often upset by violence on news programmes, 22 per cent said their child was often upset by violence in fictional programmes, 15 per cent thought television had made their child think violence is part of everyday life, and 11 per cent said their child had copied violent behaviour they had seen on television.[6]

Regulation in the form of the 9.00pm Watershed has long been used and appreciated by parents as a key indicator of the suitability of a programme for children. The majority of parents in Livingstone and Bovill's study gave overwhelming support for the Watershed with 95 per cent saying it was either a 'very good' or 'quite good' idea.[7] A Broadcasting Standards Commission study of changing public perceptions of broadcasting regulation showed that many viewers (61 per cent) think of protecting children as the main reason for regulation.[8] Whilst regulation was supported, the vast majority of respondents believed that parents rather than regulators have the prime responsibility for what children see both before and after the Watershed. A further study by the Commission (Verhulst, 2001) showed that overall, viewers see themselves as most responsible for controlling what they and other people see on television, with only 24 per cent attributing responsibility to broadcasters and programme makers, and 12 per cent to the government or regulators. However, this attitude does not necessary transpire into behaviour and Geoffrey Barlow and Alison Hill (1985) suggest that, 'evidence from many sources indicates that the influence of family example and parental control have been waning in highly developed countries for some decades.'[9] This claim appears to be supported by the conflicting reports of viewing regulation given by children and parents in Livingstone and Bovill's study. Whilst 75 per cent of mothers and 73 per cent of fathers said they tell their child when they can and cannot watch TV and videos, only 35 per cent of children reported their fathers ever doing this and 41 per cent said their mothers did this.[10] When asked whether their parents had any rules about which programmes they could watch on television, or the times of day they could watch television, 40 per cent of the 507 children on the 'YoungView' panel said they did. The proportion of children who said their parents had rules decreased as children got older, with only 21 per cent of 15-16 year olds saying their parents had rules compared to over half (55 per cent) of 10-11 year olds.[11]

Before continuing, the viewing habits of children should be considered and noted. Halloran and Gray's 1996 study showed that children's favourite programmes were Soap Operas (67 per cent) and Comedies (45 per cent) rather than Police/Thrillers (15 per cent) or Action programmes (7 per cent).[12] Children were also significantly more likely to hire videos of Comedy (53 per cent) than videos of Police/Thriller programmes (15 per cent).[13] Factual programmes such as Documentaries (20 per cent) and News (19 per cent) were disliked to a greater extent than any other programmes (apart from Soap Operas (20 per cent) which were disliked mainly by boys, and by others who disliked specific soaps such as *Neighbours* rather than the genre as a whole).[14] More recently, Livingstone and Bovill derived a list of thirteen genres from the lists of top five favourite programmes named by children in their study. The differences in favourite genres between boys and girls and different age groups are demonstrated in the table below. Most notably girls like soap operas whereas boys prefer sport, and a liking for cartoons decreases steadily with age. Whilst the distribution of preferences is not entirely consistent with Halloran and Gray's findings, both studies demonstrate an important point: children do not watch many programmes from genres that regularly feature violence and certainly do not favour such programmes.

Genre of favourite programme by gender and age

%	All	Gender		Age			
		Boy	Girl	6-8	9-11	12-14	15-17
Soap	26	11	41	11	24	33	33
Cartoon	15	20	10	36	16	6	5
Sport	14	27	2	5	14	17	21
Other series/ serial	13	8	18	12	16	13	11
Comedy	7	6	8	2	5	11	10

Source: Livingstone & Bovill (1999) Chapter 3, page 17.

The findings from David Buckingham's study (1996) suggest that parents have good reason to regulate and monitor children's viewing. He reports that children did experience feelings of fright, disgust, sadness, and worry following the viewing of violent material. It ought to be pointed out, however, that although some children did experience nightmares or a heightened fear of crime after watching violent programmes, such anguish did not appear to be long lasting or severe. When Buckingham asked the children in his study whether they were concerned about the possible effects of television, they did not consider themselves to be at risk. Some of the children did say however that they thought that younger children, who might not be able to tell the difference between fiction and reality, might be affected by violence on television. A study of children's perspectives of the potential harm caused by media conducted by the Australian Broadcasting Authority (2000) found similar opinions amongst children. One of the examples of the potential of the media to harm suggested by the children was the feelings they experience after watching horror films or supernatural films. However, they were reluctant to describe these feelings as harmful given that they also felt that watching such films was fun. Their concerns focused on the potential of such films to harm children younger than themselves, and overall they thought younger children and/or children of the opposite sex were most likely to be vulnerable to media harm. Again, it is a case of 'the other' being affected and not the respondents themselves.[15] This is an interesting finding in that if such a belief is general in the population it is not surprising that the question of the effect of television on behaviour takes on the status in the mind of the general public of an unexamined belief. It would therefore seem that violence on television is set to continue as a never-ending social concern in the manner suggested by James Halloran in his foreword to this book.

As the previous discussion of violence in factual and fictional television demonstrates, viewers do not interpret all television violence in the same way; they differentiate between various forms of violence and, in this sense, children are no different to adults. For example, Largespetz et al. (1978) showed that even children of a pre-school age were capable of distinguishing between various forms of violence and responded differently to the different forms. Largespetz et al. studied the changes in the facial expressions of pre-school children whilst they watched violent scenes in programmes portraying five different forms of violence. The types of violence were schematic violence, realistic violence in which the suffering of the victim was also shown, cartoon violence, verbal violence, and a non-violent scene. The children watched both the schematic violence and the cartoon violence with joy and understanding. They showed no signs of distress or fear. The realistic physical violence troubled the children most and was observed to have produced facial expressions of seriousness, tenseness, and anger in the children. Snow (1974) also established that pre-adolescent viewers had the ability to distinguish between real violence and fantasy violence. He found that children perceived real violence as sickening rather than frightening and that they preferred to see violence in a 'make believe' and play context which they could enjoy and subsequently forget.

Children and realist drama, crime reconstructions, and documentary

Buckingham's study (1996) suggests that 'children's emotional responses appear to depend upon complex judgements about the degree of realism in the text'.[16] Like Largespetz et al. (1978) and Snow (1974), he says that there are two forces at work in the process children use to distinguish between fact and fiction. Buckingham claims that even young children know the difference between reality and fantasy and that by the age of five or six they have an understanding of how programmes are made which becomes part of the decision process. Children make judgements about the internal formal stylistic properties of a programme when deciding whether a programme is real or not. Internal formal stylistic properties are those indicators such as the graphical conventions of cartoons that are indicative of the realistic status of a programme. Buckingham also thinks that children attribute different degrees of plausibility to a text that they know to be fictional. They use the external criteria of their own experiences and beliefs about the real world to judge whether it would be possible for a situation featured in a fictional text to happen in real life. Buckingham developed these theories from his study of children's perceptions of three programmes in which the boundary between fact and fiction was not entirely straightforward. Focus group interviews were conducted with a total of 72 children in four age groups: 6-7, 9-10, 12-13, 15-16. The three programmes were: the long running social realist hospital drama *Casualty*; the factual crime programme *Crimewatch* in which reconstructions of crimes using actors are used to try to jog viewers memories in the hope that they might volunteer useful information to the police; a one-off spoof documentary called *Ghostwatch*, broadcast on the eve of Halloween, which purported to follow a ghost hunt.

The children generally perceived *Casualty* as realist, that is, a well-constructed and accurate imitation of the real. The children knew that the action the programme was depicting was not actually happening, but thought it was a good fictional construction of what might and what does happen in the real world. The children were not scared by the programme but could recall instances from previous episodes of *Casualty* which they had found shocking or disgusting. One such instance was mentioned by a nine year old girl who said 'I thought one that wasn't particularly nice was this one with the tractor, and the man who got his leg caught in the tractor. You saw his welly boot or whatever, there was just blood pouring out.'[17] However, she was not scared by the episode, she expected such things from *Casualty*, and in fact said that she had quite enjoyed the scene. She further described how when watching *Casualty* she would look away from the screen if she knew that there was something that she did not want to see. This sort of feeling was common amongst the children who expected blood and gore from the scenes and, as Buckingham has observed with horror films, often have a positive appetite for it – 'You watch it because it's shocking ... I watch it because I know I'm going to see gory stuff, and I like it.'[18] as one 15 year old girl said. For the children, then, the realism of the programme was grounded in the internal stylistic properties of the realistic special effects and in their external perceptions of the realistic nature of the storylines. Therefore, even though the children were shocked by the blood and gore in some scenes and were sometimes upset by the storylines, such as the death of a character, these elements were central to their enjoyment of *Casualty*. Thus the series was not of great concern to them because they recognised the events portrayed to be fictional.

The majority of the children who had seen *Crimewatch* had, at some point, been scared or worried by the programme. It is interesting that many of the children said that this feeling often intensified after the programme had finished. The children felt unsafe and threatened by *Crimewatch* in the sense that it made them fearful of becoming a victim of violent crime, especially when the crimes covered in the programme were geographically close to home. For example, the girls in the sample felt especially fearful of becoming victims following exposure to this type of programme. This is a similar response to one seen earlier in Morrison and MacGregor's study (1993) when considering elderly people's responses to *Crimewatch* where the suggestion as to the base of their fear was their infirmity and thus their inability to protect themselves from violence. Both the old and the young felt vulnerable to violence through occupying extreme points of the age spectrum. It is also interesting, in light of previous observations about young female viewers' anxieties about the threat of violence to themselves, especially sexual assault, that such anxiety appears to be engendered at a very early age. In general the children found their fears difficult to cope with given that the violence seen was based on real life crime – as a 15 year-old boy said 'because it's real life, I think you get more frightened.' 'Cause you know it could just happen to anybody, which makes it more frightening. There's not really much you can do about it.'[19] The children found the reconstructions of crimes frightening because of their realism. The children considered the simplicity and lack of sensationalism in the reconstructions to be indicative of the reality of the scenes depicted – 'they don't actually have much violence, but it's more scary than a really violent film, 'cause you know it's really actually happened once.'[20] However, the upset caused by the programme appeared to be accepted by the children in much the same way as adults did in that they considered *Crimewatch* to have a valuable social purpose. Apart from its role in catching criminals, the children also thought that *Crimewatch* offered valuable lessons in crime prevention.

Ghostwatch used well known presenters and the techniques of outside broadcasting to create the impression of a documentary. Buckingham reports that the creation of the illusion of reality confused the children who watched the programme as to its actual status. Buckingham notes that the collapsing together of genres resulted in the children reporting that *Ghostwatch* was the most frightening programme they had ever seen. It is interesting that, as was also the case with *Crimewatch*, these fears were reported to have become stronger after the programme had finished. Viewers were tricked by a series of deceptions which aimed to convince the viewer that the programme was a true account of an actual ghost hunt. These included viewers phoning in to report supernatural occurrences in their own homes, and the camera panning along a curtain where a ghost like figure could be seen and quickly panning back to the curtain to give the illusion that a ghost had been identified. The programme was judged by the children to be very effective in creating the illusion of reality. The inability of the children to identify any internal contextual factors in the programme which would have suggested its fictional nature, and the belief from the children's external value system that ghosts and ghost hunts could actually exist, was a major element in the children's perception of *Ghostwatch* as real.

Children and fictional television

Van der Voort (1986)[21] showed programmes from three different fictional genre to a total of 314 children between the ages of nine and 12 in order to determine how they experienced and perceived violence in television dramas. The children watched the following programmes:

Crime Drama – *Starsky and Hutch* and *Charlie's Angels*.

Adventure Series – *Dick Turpin* and *The Incredible Hulk*.

Fantasy Cartoons – *Tom and Jerry*, *The Pink Panther*, and *Scooby Doo*.

The study found that the 'real' (Crime Drama) programmes were taken more seriously by the children and were accompanied by a higher level of emotion and a lower level of detachment than the less 'real' (Adventure Series and Cartoons) programmes. The children found the most violence in Crime Drama and the least amount of violence in Fantasy Cartoons. This is consistent with the findings of Gunter's (1985) study of adults' perceptions of violence in various fictional genre reviewed earlier.

In a further study Gunter (1988)[22] asked adults which programmes, drawn from a list of American and British Crime Dramas, they thought were suitable for children to watch. In the case of British Crime Dramas the following percentages of respondents found the programmes suitable for children: *Juliet Bravo* 72 per cent, *Bergerac* 47 per cent, *Dempsey and Makepeace* 44 per cent, and *The Bill* 33 per cent. The respondents were also asked which programmes they thought the children would not take seriously, the percentages were as follows: *Juliet Bravo* 23 per cent, *Bergerac* 40 per cent, *Dempsey and Makepeace* 42 per cent, and *The Bill* 27 per cent. Gunter points out that many viewers thought children were quite likely to take the dramas seriously, and although he fails to make it clear what he means by 'seriously' it is reasonable to presume that he means that they would find them realistic. He suggests that, with the exception of *Juliet Bravo*, the underlying reason for the respondents' reservations about the suitability of the dramas for viewing by children may be the possibility that children would perceive such programmes as realistic. He implies that the main concern of adult viewers about programmes that children take seriously was that children might watch them on their own without the supervision of an adult. Respondents were then asked similar questions about the American Crime Dramas, *The A-Team* and *The Equalizer*. Fifty per cent of the respondents agreed that *The Equalizer* was unsuitable for children and a further 38 per cent said it was likely to taken seriously by children. Most viewers (no figures given) thought that *The A-Team* was entirely suitable for young viewers. The violence featured in *The A-Team* was seen by the respondents to be based in a fantastical and humorous context. Consequently they did not think that children would take such material seriously and hence were not concerned about children watching such material whether on their own or not.

In a study of 184 children split into two age groups (4-7& 8-11), Marina Krcmar and Mark C. Cooke (2001) considered the link between children's moral reasoning and their perceptions of television violence. The study utilised theory regarding moral development to make age-based predictions about children's reactions to television violence. Using a clip from the fictional detective programme *Walker, Texas Ranger*, the researchers manipulated a violent act to create four different conditions varying by whether the violent act was punished or not, and whether there was any provocation for the violent act. The study found that 'children's age affects how they interpret the context in which violence is portrayed and that their interpretations are consistent with developmental theory related to moral reasoning'.[23] Consistent with developmental theory, they found that younger children saw unpunished violence as more justified than punished violence. This is thought to be due to younger children's greater likelihood to focus on punishment avoidance than older children. They also found that older children were more likely to have developed an ability to consider the point of view of others in their judgement of the justifiability of a violent act, and were therefore influenced by factors of provocation and motivation where younger children were not. Other studies such as that by Joanne Cantor (1994) have found that children's perceptions of frightening programmes are significantly dependent on cognitive development and whether a child will be frightened by a range of different stimuli is related to age.

Children and the news

Buckingham (1996) asked the children in his study to discuss how they felt about television news. In terms of the content of stories mentioned by the children, news reports involving innocent victims were the most frequently discussed. Issues frequently covered by the news mentioned and discussed by the children included death, physical mutilation, and cruelty to animals. Wars and disasters were also acknowledged and news items current at the time of the research – such as babies in Romanian orphanages, children killed in the former Yugoslavia, and animals being killed for trade – were raised in conversation. Buckingham observed that stories that were more geographically distant provoked feelings of sadness and pity amongst the children, whilst stories closer to home were described by them in terms of fear and personal threat. Apart from feeling sad for people suffering in far away places, such as the Romanian orphans, the children also tended to feel lucky or relieved that such a thing was unlikely to ever happen to them. These feelings were often accompanied by a sense of guilt, which some younger children sought to cope with by donating money to relevant charities. By helping to alleviate suffering through donations Buckingham claims that the children felt less guilty for being lucky, and less sad because they had at least tried to help the people who they had seen suffering. Some of the older children were of the opinion that such attempts to try to help were pointless. Their response to their own anguish caused by such reports was the straightforward one of not watching the images in question.

In news reports covering stories closer to home, and especially those covered by local news programmes, the children's perceptions of the violence shown were accompanied by fears for their own safety. Stories about rape, murder, racist violence and attacks by dangerous dogs were mentioned most often in the discussions. Buckingham comments upon how the children's observations about news reports 'often involved an imaginative "translation" from the text into the circumstance of the children's own lives.'[24] This was a particular response of the girls, who seemed to identify with victims, most often in the cases of rapes or murders of young girls, and who interpreted such events as ones which might happen to them. In the case of both boys and girls, Buckingham noted that such reportage gave rise to a fear of the dangers that might lurk outside the safety of their homes.

Coping strategies

Buckingham observed that the children found it more difficult to cope with violence witnessed in news programmes than violence that they saw in fictional programmes. He found that children employed four different strategies to cope or handle with feelings experienced as a result of viewing violence on television. These were as follows:

Partial or total avoidance of the violence – this included changing channels, turning off the television, closing their eyes until the 'bad' bits were over and hiding behind the sofa.

Changing the context of viewing – for instance, watching 'scary' programmes in the presence of others rather than on their own or at another time.

Psychological strategies – such as distracting themselves or seeking comfort.

Actively reinterpreting the text – inventing imaginary alternative endings or challenging the text's reality status.

Buckingham suggests that children apply different coping strategies to fictional violence than to factual violence. He states that children found it easier to distance themselves from violence in fictional programmes than from violence in factual programmes by reminding themselves that it was not real violence.

War news

In his study of audience opinions of television coverage of the Gulf War, David Morrison (1992) reported the opinions held by children on the subject. A sample of 212 children aged between 9 and 15 were interviewed by survey and a smaller amount took part in group discussions. A total of 51 per cent of children in the survey said they had been upset or worried by things that they had seen or heard in the television coverage of the war, but of these only a relatively small number (9 per cent) said that they had been very worried.[25] Of the 42 per cent of children who had been fairly worried and the 9 per cent who had been very worried, girls were more worried than boys by the war (of those worried, 62 per cent were girls and 43 per cent were boys).[26] Morrison suggests that 'this difference may well be accounted for in part by the fact that, as mentioned, the girls in the sample were less certain than the boys that it was right for Britain to join the other nations in the war with Iraq, and therefore

71

were more exposed to feelings of senselessness, and consequently upset, at the death and suffering that the war brought.'[27] The children were asked what had upset or worried them most about the war. Their responses were: Allied pilots/ hostages being beaten up (18 per cent), oil wells set alight/ oil spills/ wildlife at risk/dead seabirds (17 per cent), death/killing/suffering (17 per cent), worry about the war coming here/that it would last a long time (12 per cent), innocent people being killed/injured (10 per cent), and worry about possibility of friends/relatives being hurt/captured/at risk (10 per cent).[28] When the children were asked whether a particular picture or event had stuck in their minds, the most lasting image mentioned was of the pictures of the Allied airmen being paraded on television (14 per cent), followed closely by pictures of scud attacks (12 per cent) and pictures of the guided bombs (12 per cent).[29]

Coping strategies

Morrison's Gulf War study suggests that the children coped with their worries and, to a certain extent, overcame their upset by protecting themselves in the same way as adults were observed to; by reminding themselves that 'the war is a just one and therefore the misfortunes of the Iraqis are nobody's fault but that of their leader, Saddam Hussein'. However, placing the blame on the Iraqi leader did not protect the children against images of injury to the same extent that it did so for adults. The adults in Morrison's survey tended to make fatalistic statements that justified the death and injury of victims in the war as an inevitable consequence of war. The children had no such emotional protection from scenes like this and many confessed to being upset by pictures such as those of the destruction of the Amiriya bunker. Morrison observed that the children's anxieties seemed to reduce over time as the full story of the war unfolded and the children gained a fuller understanding of how the war was likely to personally affect them and their family. The children's understanding was developed through discussions about the war with friends and family as well as from the events of the war which were covered on television.

Supplementary findings

Van der Voort (1986) suggests that children watch television with a stronger level of involvement than adults. He says that as they get older (he studied 9-12 year olds) children tend to watch a greater amount of television and that their viewing habits change so that they watch fewer children's programmes and more adult programmes. He also observed that as they got older children in his study gained a better understanding of violence in television drama. Furthermore, he proposes that heavy viewers watch television differently, with the effect that they are more inclined to regard violent acts as justified than lighter viewers. He goes on to say that children who were heavy users of television were less easily frightened by violence in television programmes. However, in researching children's perceptions of violence on television Buckingham (1996) observed that children were no less upset by violence on the news when they had also watched fictional violence. What Buckingham suggests is that, regardless of how much violence children see in fictional programmes, this does not desensitise them to violence in news programmes.

Conclusions

It is evident from the reported research that children, including those as young as pre-school children, are able to distinguish between various forms of violence. For example, Van der Voort (1986) found that children did not classify the violence in cartoons as being violent. Buckingham (1996) proposes that children make a distinction between various forms of violence by considering two factors about a programme. The first factor manifests itself in the stylistic properties of a programme such as special effects and cartoon-style graphics. The second factor concerns judgements made by children about a programme that are based upon their personal experiences of the real world. In considering whether a programme is conveying a fictional or real situation children will therefore bring their external experiences of the world into the decision making process as well as making an analysis based on the textual style of the programme. When children are unable to draw any conclusions about the status of a form of violence from this process, as was the case with *Ghostwatch*, they become confused and subsequently may be distressed by acts of violence featured in the programme. Once children had made a decision as to whether a programme was real or not, they could understand and frame any violence within it. Indeed, Morrison (1992) observed that children's anxieties about violence that they saw in the television coverage of the Gulf war were reduced once they developed a fuller understanding of the events of the war through discussion with others and by watching news reports. This gradually allowed them to build up a factual basis from which to determine whether there was any direct danger to themselves or their family. In other words, worries lessened as knowledge was gained.

Notes

1 For an overview of the literature see Cumberbatch, G and Howitt, D (1989), Freedman, N (1984), Gauntlett, D (1995), Livingstone, S (1990), Potter, W.J (1999).
2 Buckingham, D (1996).
3 Broadcasting Standards Council (1996).
4 Broadcasting Standards Council (1996) p.139.
5 Broadcasting Standards Council (1996) p.139.
6 Livingstone, Sonia & Bovill, Moira (1999) Chapter 11 p.5.
7 op.cit., Chapter 11.p..25.
8 Broadcasting Standards Commission (2000a).
9 Barlow, G & Hill, A (1985).
10 Livingstone, Sonia & Bovill, Moira (1999) Chapter 11 p.17.
11 op.cit., Ch11, p.24.
12 Halloran, J.D and Gray, P (1996), p.132.
13 Halloran, J.D and Gray, P (1996), p.133.
14 Halloran, J.D and Gray, P (1996), p.134.
15 For a discussion of the 'third-person' effect in perceptions of the influence of television violence see Hoffner *et al.*(2001).
16 Buckingham, D (1996) p.213.
17 op.cit,p.219.

18 op.cit.
19 op.cit., p.230.
20 op.cit., p.234.
21 Van der Voort, T.H.A (1986).
22 Gunter, B and Wober, M (1988).
23 Krcrmar and Cooke (2001) p. 311.
24 Buckingham, D (1996.) p.194.
25 Morrison, D.E (1992) p.55.
26 op.cit., p.54.
27 op.cit., p.55.
28 op.cit., p.56.
29 op.cit., p.51.

4
Supplementary Research Findings

Fear of Crime, survivors and victims, gender, children and video games

Strictly speaking, the debate around television's influence on the audience's fear of crime is one of effects. However, in the course of reviewing research concerning the audience's perceptions of violence on television, it cannot be overlooked that fear of crime has been reported in several of the studies. In these cases fear of crime has been considered in terms of how the audience perceives violent material and how their perceptions of television crime affect their judgement of the extent of real crime and the dangers of everyday life. Because viewers' perceptions of violence in real life are held to be a consequence of perceptions of television violence, the fear of crime is of relevance to the central theme of this review.

There is widespread public concern about the level of crime in society, especially violent crime. At the end of the 1980s this anxiety was held to be so great amongst the general public that the Government saw fit to commission a working group on the fear of crime. The role of the media in the public's formation of this fear formed the central focus of the group's deliberations. The Home Office published the conclusions of the report in December 1989.[1] It stated that the public had an inflated impression of the frequency of crime, particularly violent crime, and that this impression had been created by exposure to media representations of crime. The working group's worry was that this impression of criminal activity would strengthen in the future as a result of the expected increase in the volume of media reportage of crime due to expansions in the number of available channels and the increased competition for viewers that would follow. The group suggested that programmes which they saw as being contributory to the public's fear of crime would become more common in the struggle by television channels to attract audiences. In addition to this anxiety it was implied that such programmes might report crime in an undesirable manner, by dramatising it in a way which might add to existing fears of crime. The group declared a particular concern about programmes that reported crime in the style of a reconstruction such as *Crimewatch*, *Crimestoppers*, and *Crime Monthly*. The working group concluded that an increase in such programmes would 'inevitably reinforce erroneous impressions of a major increase in violent crime, fuel fears about copycat crimes and push up the level of anxiety about individual safety.'[2] It was noted that Crime Reconstruction programmes such as those mentioned above nearly always featured unsolved crimes and in addition tended to focus on violent crime. Concern was lower in the case of lengthier reconstruction programmes such as *Crimewatch* given that such programmes were seen as providing enough time to report crimes in detail and thus present the audience with a fuller and more rounded picture of the crime that had taken place. It was held that this more in-depth treatment of a particular crime helped to allay fear of crime in a way that the more brief treatment of crime in programmes such as *Crimestoppers* was unable to do. In conclusion the working group recommended that all Crime Reconstruction programmes carry a health warning.

It is interesting that, as some of the research reviewed previously indicates (Buckingham, 1996; Morrison and MacGregor, 1993), the Home Office report stated that elderly people felt particularly afraid of crime. It was noted that media reports had intensified their fear of crime, especially those involving attacks on the elderly. Indeed the elderly people interviewed in the course of research for the report frequently mentioned that they had been frightened by photographs of badly injured faces of elderly people shown on the news. The working group concluded that those most likely to be given an exaggerated fear of crime involving violence through the portrayal of violence by the media are those people who are already afraid of crime, and those who have had least personal experience of crime.

Based on its findings the working group made several recommendations. It was proposed that editorial decisions should take account of the extent and seriousness of many people's fear of crime, and that note should be made of the way in which sensational coverage of crime can fuel fears of crime. Recommendations were made that editors should be cautious about quotes of crime statistics and references to particular crimes by politicians and pressure groups, made for their own purposes, which could often be inaccurate and misleading to the audience. There was a call from the working group for an increase in the reporting of positive stories such as crimes that had been successfully solved by the police. It was hoped that these recommendations would result in viewers gaining a more accurate perception of the risk of becoming victims of crime themselves.

Barrie Gunter (1987) questions the view that by watching violence on television the public develop an exaggerated perception of the incidence of violent crime and a subsequent greater fear of it. Gunter points out that the strength of the claim is significantly lessened when a comparison of the effects of other social forces on fear of crime is made, and when the context in which people use and react to television is considered. In addition, Gunter is particularly critical of the findings of American research that has claimed that regular viewing of violence in television dramas leads to an increased fear of crime in viewers. George Gerbner and colleagues (1976, 1978, 1979) argued that heavy users of television develop a distorted view of the world derived from portrayals of it on screen. The 'cultivation effect' theory developed by Gerbner and his colleagues claims that the more violence people watch on television, the more violence they will believe exists in society. The method Gerbner *et al.* used in developing the cultivation theory has been criticised for several reasons.

First, the theory is based entirely on basic correlations made between levels of viewing and levels of anxiety about crime. Gerbner et al. concluded that when both levels of viewing and fear of crime are high the fear felt by viewers is produced solely by the viewing of television violence.[3] Gunter and others make criticisms of the assumption by Gerbner *et al.* that heavy viewing of television violence leads to an exaggerated fear of crime. Doob & McDonald (1989) and Mallory Wober and Barrie Gunter (1982) argue that the research does not take sufficient account of the influence of social factors other than television on viewers' perceptions of television violence. These factors include the age, sex, social class, level of education, area of residence and psychological dispositions of viewers. It has been observed that when these factors are controlled for along with other variables the relationship that Gerbner *et al.* found between the level of television viewing and perceptions of crime is considerably weakened. Gunter (1987) also suggests that it would be wrong to base assumptions about fear of crime on the *amount* of television that people watch and that it would be more accurate to consider *which* programmes people with a high fear of crime watch. Gunter bases this statement on the theory that viewers' judgements about real life crime are influenced more heavily by violence viewed in factual programmes than that which is seen in fictional programmes. Indeed, where fear of crime is mentioned in the research reviewed in previous chapters it is nearly always with reference to one particular programme. For instance, some of the children in Buckingham's study (1996) had become fearful of becoming victims of crime after watching the Crime Reconstruction programme *Crimewatch*. The children's perceptions were observed to be more influenced by real life crime in factual programmes as opposed to crime featured in fictional programmes. Gunter's (1987) main criticism of Gerbner's theory is that it fails to address three questions which Gunter believes are vital in determining what causes viewers to have an increased fear of crime: do viewers perceive television to be violent? do viewers generalise that television reflects the real world? do individuals who perceive the real world as violent also have a greater fear of crime? Therefore, in much the same way that the public debate about the effect of televised violence on viewers is centred around a concern that is not grounded in any firm evidence, the consequences of television violence on the extent to which viewers have a fear of crime also requires rigorous examination.

Indeed, this call for rigorous sociological empirical investigation features strongly in James Halloran's account of his establishment of the Leicester Centre in the early days of British mass communications research.

Survivors and violence in factual programming

In *Survivors and the Media* (1991) Ann Shearer explains the findings of two studies into the attitudes of both survivors and relatives of survivors of violent crime or disasters to the portrayals of violence on television. The research was based on a survey of 1,050 people (one fifth of whom happened to have survived an act of violence) and in-depth interviews with 54 people selected through Victim Support agencies. The latter group had encountered violence either as a survivor of a major disaster, car accident, murder, rape or other instances of violence, or had lost a relative in such circumstances. In order to avoid confusion, the respondents from the survey will be referred to as 'the survey respondents' and the respondents from the in-depth interviews will be referred to as 'the survivors'. It must also be pointed out that although some of the respondents from the survey had survived a violent incident, Shearer does not distinguish their responses from the rest of the survey group who had not experienced any violence. Although the survivors were not always asked precisely the same questions as those posed in the survey, the research nevertheless does allow comparisons to be made between the two groups.

Shearer considers the survivors to be a minority group of the population as a whole because they had all suffered the effects of relatively rare instances of violence. She researched their opinions about the media's role in the reporting of their experiences. Some of the survivors referred to the possible positive roles that the media can play. In some cases survivors found that the chance to tell their story in the media was an important part of the healing process. Furthermore, in cases involving possible miscarriages of justice, the media was seen as responsible for keeping the issue alive and prompting authorities to investigate the circumstances around the incident. For example, the media was seen to have played a major role in pushing for safety regulations in football grounds following the Hillsborough stadium disaster.[4] In cases of major disasters Shearer points out that the media is usually the public's first source of news about the event and helps to ensure that friends and relatives know how to find out more information by contacting named authorities. However, the survivors did not overlook the perceived negative role of the media. Although most complaints about the role of the media in covering disasters or violent incidents and accidents were directed at the press, the broadcast media were also criticised for the distress they can cause by the manner of their reports. Shearer found that there are four main elements that can distress survivors: timing, intrusion and harassment, inaccuracy and distortion, and detail.

Although it was usually the press or radio that were named as the culprits of bad timing, a source of anxiety with regard to all media was that the names of victims might be released before relatives had been informed. Shearer concludes that unless there is a disaster following which relatives need to know quickly whom to contact for further information, the names of victims should not be released before the relatives of the victims have first been contacted. Distressed and bereaved people did not want cameras intruding into their privacy, especially at funerals or at their home. Survivors wanted reports to be accurate because even errors in the reporting of relatively minor facts such as age were found to be extremely upsetting to people who were already distressed. There were also concerns about the propensity of editing to give an inaccurate picture of the event taken as a whole or to distort people's comments by quoting them out of context. Although this may be a common criticism of editing it must be borne in mind that, in the case of disasters or incidents which result in violent death, survivors or relatives of the deceased are unusually sensitive to the manner in which such reports are framed: for them the news is a personal tragedy. Another major worry was that too much detail in a report might lead to the victim's identity or address being identifiable.

Both survivors and survey respondents were asked to say how acceptable they found ten hypothetical news items to be. Shearer notes that to her surprise there was a high level of agreement between the groups. Both groups found items that covered the harsh reality of tragedy least acceptable. The two least acceptable items for both groups were: (1) the scene of a major incident showing dead or seriously injured people who are recognisable, and (2) pictures of people who have been bereaved and are in a very emotional state. The views of the groups only differed significantly in the case of one scene which featured the funeral of a victim of a terrorist attack. The survey respondents generally found it acceptable (66 per cent), although the women in the survey were less likely to approve of it than the men. There was disagreement amongst the survivors, but they rejected it as unacceptable by a narrow margin (no figure given).[5] The research also showed that the survivors and the survey respondents generally agreed on the types of items that could be shown before the Watershed. People opted in most instances for selected pictures with commentary pre-Watershed rather than full coverage.

Both groups were also asked to consider how acceptable they found dramatic reconstructions of violence such as last sightings of murder victims or missing persons (questions posed to the survivors) and violent crimes and natural disasters (questions posed to the survey respondents). Unfortunately because the two sample groups were not asked to consider the same reconstructions their responses are not directly comparable. Within the survivors group there was disagreement over how much coverage should be shown in the early evening, but after the Watershed 26 out of 38 opted for full coverage.[6] The survey respondents did not discuss the timing of the reconstructions, but the results did show that people who had themselves been victims found reconstructions of violent crimes slightly more acceptable (66 per cent) than those who had not (59 per cent).[7]

In a part of Shearer's study involving only the survivors, three different ways of reporting four different situations, each varying in explicitness, were discussed. These were rape, the murder of children, major traffic accidents and the Hillsborough disaster. Given that the reactions of the survivors to the different styles of reporting were similar in each case, it is possible to describe the findings of the research through one of the examples. The outcome from the discussion of the various ways of covering the Hillsborough tragedy accurately conveys the perceptions of the survivors to such types of reporting in general. In each case the three scenarios varied in detail from explicit visual images of the situation to verbally descriptive reports. The Hillsborough scenarios were as follows:

(1) Film and voice over of events as they happened with detailed shots of the victims.

(2) Reports after the event, with pictures of the football ground and interviews with survivors.

(3) A factual report of what happened, how many died, and what is being done to prevent another disaster. Pictures of the situation by air.

Disgust was the reaction to the first scenario. It was deemed totally unsuitable. As one person said, 'Disgusting. ... I know of people who saw their children suffocating on television.'.[8] Scenario two was more widely accepted but there was a division of opinion about the interviews with survivors. The final scenario, although thought by all to be acceptable in terms of the level of violence, was seen as inadequate in conveying the magnitude of the disaster. Respondents said it was too detached and lacked impact. In general, and with regard to the other situations considered, most people did not approve of the most detailed style of report but found that a less detailed factual report did not adequately convey the nature of the event.

Three conclusions came out of the research: (1) reports should cause minimum distress to survivors, relatives and others who have suffered tragedies; (2) it is only acceptable to cause distress if reports have a use and a purpose; (3) control should be exercised over what is reported. On a more basic level the research showed that live coverage of an event and material which reveals the identity of the victim or where they live is distressing and as such completely unacceptable to survivors as viewers.

Women and violence on television

Phillip Schlesinger *et al.* (1992) studied the perceptions of a group of women whose backgrounds varied in terms of experience of violence, social class, age, national background (Scottish/English) and ethnicity (16 per cent Afro-Caribbean, 31 per cent Asian, and 53 per cent White). In total 91 women were shown scenes depicting violence against women from four different programme genres. Just over half of the women in the sample had previously experienced some form of violence, usually in the home at the hands of a male partner. The programmes shown to the groups were divided into the following genres:

A factual Crime Reconstruction programme, *Crimewatch* – including the reconstruction of the rape and murder of a young woman.

A prime time Soap Opera with a strong social issues orientation, *EastEnders* – the edition shown featured scenes of domestic violence.

A one-off play made by a documentarist, *Closing Ranks* – the key theme of the drama was marital violence.

An American feature film first released in the cinema then shown on television and made available on video, *The Accused* – the film included a scene in which a woman was subjected to gang rape.

The study aimed to determine the possible differential perceptions of violence as a determinant of the different backgrounds of the women and the differences between them in terms of exposure to real life violence. The researchers observed that an experience of the type of violence portrayed in the programmes was the most significant differentiating factor among the viewers in accounting for their responses to the violence shown. Whilst there were few noteworthy differences between the classes, ethnicity, however, did make a difference. First, some women from ethnic groups were critical of the portrayal of their own ethnic group in some of the programmes. For instance, the Afro-Caribbean women accused *EastEnders* of making what they saw as racist statements about mixed marriages and the negative comment about the general social competence of black women. They also disapproved of what they saw as the singling out of black criminals by *Crimewatch*. Second, some members of ethnic groups felt so alienated from the white culture displayed in the programmes, that they felt unable to comment on some of the violent scenes shown. They found that the cultural world within which the violence occurred was so removed from theirs that they had a great deal of difficulty identifying with it at an empathetic level. This was particularly the case with the Asian women's perceptions of the film *The Accused*, which featured a gang rape scene in a bar. Totally unaccustomed to the drinking hall or bar, they could not situate the scene in any meaningful context.

Notwithstanding these responses from members of the groups from ethnic minorities, those viewers who had experienced violence in real life were 'more sensitive to televised violence, more subtle and complex in their readings, more concerned about the possible effects and more demanding in their expectations of the producers.'[9] Of the women with personal experience of violence, between half and all of them were able to relate to the characters or situations portrayed by the programmes apart from those in the film *The Accused* which was something of an exception. Only one third of the women could identify with the female victim within the film. As with the case of the women from ethnic minority backgrounds, although to a lesser degree, the extent to which the women identified with the character was limited by the gulf between their own culture and that of the character – the scene was set in a 'low life'

American bar. In contrast, of the women without experience of personal violence, only one third or less related to either the characters or the situations in the four programmes shown.

Although the research showed that the women's perceptions were influenced and divided by their ethnic background and life experience, there were similarities amongst the sample based on the commonalty of gender. Thus, similarities in the women's interpretations of the violence in the programmes were a derivative of their life experiences as *women*, such as the relationships between women and men and the women's affective relationships with others, particularly children. It is noted in the study that perceptions of the rape and murder featured in *Crimewatch* and even the gang rape depicted in *The Accused*, despite the earlier qualification, were the same for all the women, regardless of any differentiating factors, and that includes experience of violence. Schlesinger *et al.* account for this by suggesting that there is an inherent fear amongst *all* women of male sexual violence, especially attacks by strangers, and that rape was therefore a concern common to all of the sample. However, women in the sample who had experienced violence were more sensitive and fearful of the domestic sexual violence portrayed in *EastEnders* and *Closing Ranks* than those who had no such experience. Accordingly, the researchers propose that violent portrayals of rape and murder are worrying to all women regardless of life experience, class or ethnicity, but that scenes of domestic violence are of more concern to those women whose fears and memories of their own personal experience of such violence are likely to be re-activated by violent domestic scenes.

A strong conclusion of the research was therefore that the women's perceptions of violence on television were partly determined by the level of their fears about themselves becoming a victim of such violence. Schlesinger *et al.* point out that, although statistically it is more likely that women will suffer domestic violence than be raped by a stranger, it was the possibility of the latter that instilled the most fear and hence a high level of disturbance when viewing such acts. It could be argued, if it is accepted that violence on television *does* contribute to the fear of crime, that the incidence of representation of rape on television, at least in factual programmes, is much greater than domestic violence due to the attention it is awarded by the News and Crime Reconstruction programmes, and that this is a contributing factor in women's fear of rape. Domestic violence is more often a feature of fictional programmes than factual programmes and even then is not as heavily featured as rape.

In accounting for fear of violence, viewers perceptions of violence are more important than the actual probability of the occurrence of violence. Schlesinger *et al.* conclude that gender operates in certain ways to shape women's perceptions of televised violence; it differentiates women from men, and in terms of women's concerns about sexual violence from strangers, gender is a factor that cuts across class, ethnicity, and previous experience of violence. However, the perpetration of domestic violence against women separates some women from others in terms of experience and hence perception in a way that is not the case for men.

Men viewing violence

As a follow up to the 1992 study *Women Viewing Violence*, in 1996 the Broadcasting Standards Commission commissioned a team from Stirling Media Research Institute and the Violence Research Centre, Manchester University, to study how different representations of violence on television are perceived by men (Schlesinger *et al.*, 1998). Following a similar design to the previous study of women, fifteen focus groups were conducted with a total of 88 men between the ages of 18 and 75. The men were recruited from varying backgrounds according to social status, ethnicity (71 per cent white, 17 per cent Pakistani, 9 per cent Afro-Caribbean, 3 per cent West African),[10] experience of violence and, in addition to the variables considered in the study of women, age and sexual orientation. Although over half of the sample had either been attacked in a public place (53 per cent) or had been in a fight (36 per cent), the men did not categorise themselves as victims of violence, and few had been attacked in their own homes (8 per cent).[11] Therefore, unlike the study of women, the groups were not strictly constituted on the basis of the men's experience of violence. However, the men were asked to consider how their encounters with violence might influence their perceptions of televised violence.

The groups were shown a broader range of violent scenes than those used in the previous study. For example, in order to accommodate the differences between men's and women's viewing preferences, sport was included in the sample of clips shown. The selection of programmes was also expanded to incorporate both violence against women and violence against men. The following programmes were shown to the groups (N.B. ★ = programmes shown to all groups):

A soap opera with social issues, *EastEnders* – the episode dealt with the issue of one of the main male character's alcoholism and included some discussion of violence against women and children.★

A realistic drama, *Trip Trap*, featuring violence against a wife and the rape of a female neighbour set in the context of middle-class family life.

A factual documentary, *When the Fighting Starts*, based on CCTV footage of a violent attack on a young man in a public setting.★

A Hollywood action film, *Under Siege*, featuring highly stylised, 'comic book' violence dominated by a central heroic male character.

Two televised boxing matches – (1) A fight between Nigel Benn vs. Gerald McClellan which displayed elements of drama and brutality; (2) A fight between Prince Naseem Hamed vs. Remigio Molina epitomising the glamorous nature of boxing promoted by Satellite television.★

Footage of the footballer Eric Cantona's kung-fu kick against a supporter of a rival team.★

In keeping with the assumptions underlying the previous work with women, the study considered the role that gender, social status, ethnicity and experience of violence might play in affecting attitudes to on-screen violence. The aim therefore was to explore the way in which the men's perceptions of televised violence were differentiated by these determinants and, in addition, to compare the men's reactions with those of women in the 1992 study.

Overall, in comparison to the women, the men appeared to be less involved with the issues and situations portrayed in the programmes, and displayed a low level of engagement with the characters and individuals shown, especially in the fictional portrayals of domestic violence. The men did not find it necessary, as the women had, to explore the reasons and motivations of the characters involved in domestic violence. Furthermore, whereas the women often demonstrated an empathy with all the characters involved, especially the females, the men expressed no feelings of sympathy with any of the characters, and had no interest in trying to understand the feelings of the female characters who were victims of violence. Although the men condemned the violent behaviour of the husband in *Trip Trap*, and disapproved of violence against women in general, they did not view such violence with the same level of involvement and concern as women in the previous study had.

It is likely that, due to their lack of experience of domestic violence and their ability to disregard the threat of themselves becoming victims of such violence, the men were unable to relate to the situations shown. Thus, they were not as sensitive to televised violence as the women had been, especially when compared to those women who themselves had been victims of domestic violence. Although many of the men in the groups had experienced violence, the fact that they did not perceive themselves as victims of violence was fundamental to their perceptions of on-screen violence. Furthermore, the non-existence of an underlying belief that they themselves might become a victim of violence meant that, for the majority of the men, none of the violence shown to them, factual or fictional, invoked any of feelings of fear of experiencing such violence and accordingly, they were not distressed by any of the material shown. This contrasts starkly with one of the main findings of the research with women all of whom, regardless of experience of violence, class or ethnicity, found violent portrayals of rape and murder worrying. Schlesinger *et al.* account for this by reference to a basic fear that the women had of themselves becoming victims of such violence. Indeed, those women who had been victims of domestic violence were influenced by their experience and were more likely to be concerned about scenes portraying domestic violence than those women who had not been victims. It should not be overlooked, however, that fears about becoming a victim of violence were mentioned by a few of the respondents in the male study. For example, gay men found the attack in *When the Fighting Starts* unsettling and were especially sensitive to abusive situations. Schlesinger *et al* suggest that the gay men's responses were influenced by their personal experience of violence, as well as a more general underlying feeling of being members of a victimised minority group. The responses of gay men also differed from the other men in terms of their greater propensity to empathise with female characters such as 'Kathy' in *EastEnders* who was the victim of domestic violence. But, as previously mentioned, the majority of the men were not interested in exploring the feelings of the characters involved in violence, especially women.

In line with the findings of other research reported in earlier chapters, Schlesinger *et al.* found that the men drew clear distinctions between factual and fictional programmes and that violence featured in factual programmes had a greater impact upon them than fictional violence. For instance, the real life fight shown in the documentary *When the Fighting Starts* induced a high level of engagement with the issues covered. Indeed, this was the only programme out of those shown which provoked any comments by the men about televised violence invoking feelings of fear of becoming a victim of violence. The other factual depictions of violence shown to the groups involved boxing and an incident from a football match. In general, the men accepted that aggression and violence was part and parcel of televised sport and accepted it as the norm. However, some concerns were raised by middle aged men over the show business type coverage of boxing by Sky television. They felt that glamorising the sport covered up the brutal and dangerous reality of boxing. Both groups of gay men expressed a dislike for boxing, not only finding the sport 'sickening', but in addition they felt that the violent spectacle could incite viewers both in public and at home to behave violently. However, most men found the violence and subsequent injuries justifiable when they considered the professional nature of the sport and the choice of those involved to undertake such risks. The majority of the men found Cantona's violent attack on the football fan unacceptable. Although they recognised that he was provoked, they did not consider his actions to be justified and felt that his position as a role model for children made his actions even less tolerable. Whilst the men from ethnic minorities were more likely to sympathise with Cantona as a victim of racism, they did not condone his action.

The fictional violence shown to the men which they classified as realistic had a greater impact upon them than that which they saw as unrealistic. For instance, the men found the realism of scenes of domestic violence in *Trip Trap*, which included rape, uncomfortable. In contrast, they dismissed the violence in *Under Siege* and *Basic Instinct* as unrealistic, describing it as 'total fantasy' 'laughable' and 'not to be taken seriously'.[12] Many of the younger men readily admitted to enjoying this type of violence, but some of the older men disapproved of using violence as entertainment.

As in *Women Viewing Violence* Schlesinger *et al.* found ethnicity to be a differentiating factor in the perceptions of the violence viewed. In the same way that Asian women were unable to situate the rape scene in *The Accused* in any meaningful context, the Pakistani men found it difficult to identify with the storyline of alcoholism in *EastEnders*. They saw alcohol as an undesirable part of dominant culture, antipathetic to their Muslim beliefs and pointed out the initiating role of alcohol in many violent situations. Indeed, they saw drink as the primary reason for the violence in *When the Fighting Starts*. The West African men voiced similar concerns about the relationship between drinking and violence which they saw as an unappealing aspect of British culture. Independently of their views on violence, both Pakistani and Afro-Caribbean men expressed concern about the stereotypical treatment and/or lack of representation of people from ethnic minorities in *EastEnders* and other programmes. Similar criticisms were made by women from ethnic minorities in the earlier study.

Because of differences in samples and materials used, it is not possible to make direct comparisons between the two studies. Nonetheless Schlesinger *et al.* note that gender plays a major role in differentiating viewers' perceptions of television violence. The men's reactions and discussions of the violence shown differed in several ways from those of the women. Some of these differences such as sympathy with characters, level of engagement with programmes, and fear of becoming a victim of violence have already been discussed. The women in the 1992 study tended to draw on their experiences of collective viewing when discussing programmes, especially viewing rape scenes in the company of men. They also talked about how other people, such as children, would react to the violence shown, and voiced concerns over the possible consequences of such material. In contrast, the men restricted their comments to how they themselves responded to material and did not discuss how others might respond. In discussing the portrayals of rape, women condemned all forms of rape, regardless of the circumstances. However, the men were ambivalent in their attitudes to the rape scenes in *Trip Trap* and *Basic Instinct*. They showed little sympathy for the victim in *Trip Trap* and they questioned whether the sex in *Basic Instinct* was consensual or rape.

Schlesinger *et al's* study of men supported their judgement, based on their earlier research with women, that gender is a major differentiating factor in viewers' perceptions of violence. A major finding of the studies was that the primary difference between men' and women's perceptions of screen violence is women's view of themselves as potential victims of violence. Men did not see themselves as being at risk of becoming victims of violence, and in particular did not see themselves at risk from sexual violence from strangers in the same way that women did. Furthermore, unlike the women, an experience of violence was not a discriminating influence in the men's perceptions of on-screen violence in any significant way. Age, ethnicity and sexual orientation shaped differences in interpretations of violence.

Children and violence in video games

In recent years the public's concern about the possible negative effects of violence on television has expanded to embrace violence in video games. The term 'video games' originated in the late 1970s to describe the video machines that children could play in arcades. The term is now used to describe the games available to children to play at home on personal computers and, more commonly, on separate systems linked to televisions, such as the Sony 'Playstation' or 'Nintendo'. Technological development has meant that the sophisticated nature of the graphics now available is rapidly approaching near photographic quality. This is significant in the light of research findings which show that violence is a major theme of video games. For example, Patricia Greenfield (1984) noted that most video games in arcades had themes of personal aggression. More recently Eugene F. Provenzo (1991) reported that 40 out of 47 (85 per cent) of the most popular video games had violence as their major theme. In his research Victor Strasburger (1995) described the violent content of five of the most popular video games on the market in September 1993. These were:

Mortal Kombat – There were two versions of this game available. The first version was described as violent, but not gory, and the second version, which was not censored by the manufacturers' so called 'blood code', was violent and exceptionally gory. In the gory version the player could either decapitate or rip out the heart of the opponent if he/she won.

Night Trap – Vampires attack scantily clad women. If the vampires are not defeated, they drill through the women's necks with a power tool.

Lethal Enforcers – Players fire a large pistol at the screen to kill various targets.

Splatterhouse 3 – A man wearing a hockey mask uses a meat cleaver and knife to try to save his family from flesh eating monsters.

Terminator 2 – The player shoots at threatening androids with a machine gun, a rocket launcher and a shotgun.

Strasburger notes that the conflict in these games could only be resolved by competition, aggression, and death. A teacher interviewed in the course of James Halloran and Peggy Gray's (1996) research into young people and the media expressed a similar opinion, 'Games (video games) are about fighting and killing – you progress by killing, slaying or defeating, that's how you get where you want to go. It's an abstract concept, kill someone to succeed, but it has a message about dispensability.'[13] Furthermore, Kindler (1991) suggests that violent video games reinforce a notion in children that violence is a common aspect of everyday culture and that pleasure is gained from inflicting violence. The concern is clearly that by showing children that the way to win in video games is through violence, children may learn to accept violence as a way of conflict resolution and as an inevitable part of everyday life. This concern about video violence is really little different in its essential component to the concern over violence on television in general, the main difference being the medium of delivery and the accessibility of such material. Having said that however, there is one important difference, namely that video game violence is interactive. The video game player is more than just a viewer, he or she is a player of violence, an active participant who uses their own skills to make violence unfold.

Although very little is known about children's perceptions of violence in video games, or about the effect of violence in video games on children's behaviour, there is research that claims to demonstrate that children's aggression levels increase after playing video games. For example, Greenfield (1984) quotes the work of Silvern, Willhamson and Countermine (1983)[14] as evidence that violent video games produce violent behaviour in children. Silvern *et al.* found that the level of aggressive play in five year old children increased after they had played the video games *Space Invader* and *Roadrunner*. Other research has also found that aggression and hostility increased in children during free play after playing video games (Mehrabian and Wixen 1986, Cooper and Mackie 1987).[15] Greenfield proposes that the reason video games lead to increased aggression in children is that the games involve very little social interaction due to their solitary playing status. Based on two studies, Craig Anderson and Karen Dill (2000) also claim that violent video games cause aggression, and furthermore that they might have a more harmful effect than violence on television. They suggest that due to the interactive and engrossing nature of video games players are required to identify with the aggressor. In an article in the *New Scientist* Guy Cumberbatch (2000) is critical of their study. Whilst he accepts that the results do show a 'reasonably strong association between the playing of video games and concurrent aggressive behaviour and delinquency,' he criticises the research because 'it tells us nothing about causal relationships: are video games the root of the problem or the cause of it?'.[16] Similarly, in a comprehensive review of empirical studies of the relationship between violence in video games and aggression, Mark Griffiths (1999) concludes 'the question of whether video games promote aggressiveness cannot be answered at present because the available literature is relatively sparse and conflicting, and there are many different types of video games which probably have very different effects.'[17]

Jeffery Goldstein (1994)[18] argues that children do not perceive violence in video games in the same way that they perceive violence on television. Indeed, he argues that video violence is not as likely as television violence to have negative consequences. Goldstein acknowledged that video games designed for one player do not involve any social interaction, and thus can lead to heightened levels of aggression in children, but he points out that two-player games involve co-operation among players and thus do not increase levels of aggression. He goes on to suggest that a possible explanation of increased aggression after viewing television violence may be because it does not involve any social interaction with other people. It should be noted however, that this theory can only be accepted, even on its own terms, as offering an explanation for aggression following exposure to violence on television if people watch alone, because television is commonly viewed with other people, and consequently verbal interaction frequently occurs not just post viewing, but also during viewing of programmes. It should also be noted at this point that the concept that watching portrayals of violence leads to imitation or increases in aggression is a far from settled issue in the social sciences as the literature reviews of studies in this area clearly show.[19] Goldstein is at pains to point out what he considers to be the difference between the likely effect of video violence and television violence by noting that the abstract unrealistic fantasy level of video game violence is not so easily learned or imitated by children as the more realistic violence shown in television. Goldstein's final point is that video games are an interactive medium allowing the player to control what takes place on the screen and in turn players can control their own emotional states. Dolf Zillmann (1991) described how players of video games are able to 'play with the degree of involvement and activity which is most pleasing to them.'[20] Therefore, these researchers argue that children can control their experience of violence in video games in a way that is not possible with television.

Notes

1   Home Office (1989).
2   Home Office (1989), p.32.
3   For an in depth critique of the conclusions made by Gerbner et al. see Gauntlett, D (1995).
4   Ninety six football fans died as a result of a crush on the terraces at Sheffield Wednesday's Hillsborough football ground on 15 April 1989.
5   Shearer, Ann (1991) p.37.
6   op.cit, p.40.
7   op.cit, p.40.
8   op.cit, p.41.
9   Schlesinger, P. *et al.* (1992).
10 Schlesinger, P. *et al.* (1998).
11 op.cit, p.74.
12 op.cit, p.48.
13 Broadcasting Standards Council (1996), p.57.
14 Silvern, S, Willhamson, P, & Countermine, T (1983).
15 Mehrabian & Wixen 1986, Cooper & Mackie 1987 in Strasburger, V.C (1995).
16 Cumberbatch, G (2000).
17 Griffiths, M(1999), p.211.
18 Goldstein, J.H (1994.).
19 For further reference see Freedman, N (1984), Cumberbatch, G and Howitt, D (1989), Gauntlett, D (1995), Livingstone, S (1990) and Potter, W.J (1999).
20 Zillman (1991) in Goldstein, J,H (1994).

5
Research in other countries

Concern about the possible effects on viewers of violence on television is not a worry unique to the British public: the same concerns manifest themselves in other countries. However, it is worth noting that concern is higher in the USA than elsewhere, and that concern about civil violence is probably higher in America than elsewhere. Whatever the connection or non-connection between screen violence and real life violence, the concern about the possibility of a connection has resulted in more literature in the area of effects of television being produced in America than in any other country. The following section briefly reviews various enquiries into media in countries other than Britain that have addressed audience perceptions of violence on television.

Australia

The Australian National Committee on Violence, 1995
The Committee concluded that violence on television plays a minor role in comparison to other social factors in contributing to violent behaviour in viewers and violent crime. At the same time the Committee did concede, 'television violence may produce attitude changes, prove justification for violence and suggest that problems can be solved through aggressive behaviour.'[1]

Reports by the Australian Broadcasting Authority

Children and Media Harm, 2000
The study was based on focus groups with children and was wide ranging in its coverage of children's perspectives on media harm. It considered three main issues:

Who did the children consider were vulnerable to media harm and why.

The ideas the children had about the nature of media harm, and the concerns of adults.

The opinions they have about the changing nature of the media and how it challenges their established notions of harm and their strategies for dealing with media harm.

Children claimed that it was younger children and/or children of the opposite sex who were vulnerable to media harm, and older children considered themselves capable of controlling their own viewing. As in other studies reviewed earlier, the children believed that the high impact of dramatic violence was outweighed by their knowledge that it was not 'real' and the impact of violence in documentary was intensified by its reality. The children felt that many parents were vague or inept at explaining the potential harm from media, and the most concrete evidence of harm they could suggest was feeling scared after watching a horror film. Instead, the children suggested 'real life' risks and dangers as the forms of harm most relevant to them.

Your Say: A Review of audience concerns about Australia's broadcast media, 1996
This annual report asked the Australian public similar questions to those asked of the British public in the Independent Television Commission's publication "Television: The Public's View".[2] These included questions on the offensiveness and acceptability of television programmes. The main findings concerning violence on television were as follows:

— Violence was less acceptable than swearing, nudity and sex scenes.

— 71 per cent said there was too much violence in films starting at 8.30 pm on commercial television.

— 38 per cent had seen something on television over the last 8 months which caused offence or which they found unacceptable. Apart from items in the news and current affairs programmes, other major concerns over the portrayal of violence were in the realm of drama series/serials, content of advertising, and movies.

'Cool' or 'gross': Children's attitudes to violence, kissing, and swearing on television, 1994
This research monograph reported on the concerns children have about violence, kissing, nudity and swearing on television. The results from the research report on children's perceptions of violence on television were:

— 55 per cent of children said that they had stopped watching television, on occasion, because something had upset them. Of those, 50 per cent categorised their upset under the heading of violence which included animals being hurt or killed and people being killed.

— 45 per cent of parents said their children were most upset by television depiction's and portrayals of real life happenings (40 per cent said violence).

— 48 per cent of parents said that they regulated programmes or content related to violence.

— The type of violence portrayed in a programme influenced the way the children reacted to programmes.

Classification Issues: Film, Video, & Television, 1993

The research aimed to assess community standards with regard to television, film and video classification. The findings of the research showed that the issue of most concern to the population was violence, with 65 per cent believing that violence in society was linked to violence on television. However, one third of the respondents reported enjoying films containing violence. Women were more concerned about violence than men, but there was a universal view held by women and men that explicit scenes of rape and sexual violence ought not to be shown on television at any time (72 per cent).

Reports by the Australian Broadcasting Tribunal

Sex, Violence and Offensive Language: Community Views on Classification of Television Programmes, 1991

This research monograph aimed to explore public attitudes to classification issues such as sex, violence and offensive language. The main concerns about violence reported by the monograph were:

— Violence was a concern for a greater proportion of survey respondents than were the other classification issues of sex, offensive language and nudity.

— 29 per cent of adults spontaneously mentioned violence as an aspect of television which particularly concerned them.

— When prompted, 78 per cent were either 'quite' or 'very' concerned about the amount of violence on television.

— With both the prompted and unprompted responses, women were more likely than men to indicate concern about violence on television. In addition, concern about violence on television increased with age and was stronger among parents than among people without children.

Television Violence in Australia: Report to the Minister for Transport and Communications, 1990

The report was commissioned by the Australian Ministry for Transport and Communications. It is particularly interesting in that it reports very similar findings to much of the research previously covered by this review.

— In general, the extent to which televised violence is considered to be a problem and the degree of tolerance towards its presentation is strongly related to the key demographic variables of age, sex and parenthood. The level of concern about violence on television was particularly high among certain groups: the elderly, women, parents, and people with strong religious beliefs.

— People discriminated between different types of violence: 51 per cent believed there were circumstances where it was justifiable to show violence. These circumstance included: news (46 per cent) and real life events (31 per cent).

– The degree and strength of concern expressed increased significantly in situations where violence was presented in a news or current affairs context compared to the fictional context of a film or drama series.

– The more realistic, explicit and personally relevant the violence, the more likely it was to have a significant emotional impact on the audience.

– Younger people were more inclined to accept contextual justifications for violence in the demands of storyline. However, young people were still likely to get upset by violence which they could personally identify with.

– More than 70 per cent of adults saw children as the group most likely to be affected by television violence. The most reported effect of the portrayal of violence on screen was perceived to be a growing acceptance of violence as a normal part of everyday life and/or desensitisation to violence.

USA

The American Psychological Association (APA) Commission On Youth & Violence

The Commission held the view that high levels of viewing violence on television contribute to an increased acceptance of aggressive attitudes and aggressive behaviour.

The Commission reported that in response to television violence attitudes and behaviour towards violence were altered in the following ways:

Fear of crime – viewers' fears of becoming victims of violence caused them to participate in self-protective behaviours and to have a greater mistrust of others.

Desensitisation – viewers developed a callous attitude to violence and were less likely to help victims of violence.

Appetite for violence – viewers were likely to have an increased desire to become involved with or to expose themselves to violence.

The Commission concluded by saying that children could be taught 'critical viewing' skills at school and at home and that television can be 'an effective and persuasive teacher of pro-social attitudes and has the potential to make a major contribution towards reducing violence.'

'National Television Violence Study' (1996, 1997, 1998) conducted by a research consortium of North American Universities

The National Television Violence Study was a three-year effort funded by the National Cable Television Association and involving studies by four American Universities. The University of California, Santa Barbara, provided a content analysis of violence in series, daytime television, daytime movies, specials, children's shows and music videos. The University of Texas, Austin, conducted research on violence in 'reality' programmes. The University of Wisconsin, Madison, undertook a study of how ratings and advisories are used on television and the role of different types of ratings and advisories in the viewing habits of children. The University of North Carolina, Chapel Hill, provided an analysis of the effectiveness of anti-violence public service announcements and educational initiatives of the television industry. The issues that the study aimed to address were:

–   Among the various ways in which violence can be depicted, which types of portrayals have been shown through scientific research to increase the risk of problematic effects on audiences, such as imitation, fear and desensitisation?

–   What is the extent of violence on television? More importantly, how much violence is portrayed in ways that increase the risk of problematic effects on audiences?

–   Where and when do problematic portrayals of violence occur? Are there particular genres of programming, times of day, or types of channel, that contain higher or lower levels of problematic portrayals?

–   Do various ratings and advisories affect the risk that vulnerable audiences, such as adolescents and children, will be exposed to problematic portrayals of violence?

–   How can anti-violence messages, such as public service announcements, be best designed to help de-glamorise violence?

The results of some of this research were reviewed earlier in the book with reference to violence in fictional television.

Notes

1   'The Australian National Committee on Violence' in Gulbenkian Foundation (1995).
2   Annual publication produced by the ITC. Published by John Libbey, London from 1992 onwards (published in previous years by the IBA and the ITA).

6
Overview

Overall the research reviewed found that viewers' perceptions of violence on television are varied and complex. Several elements of violence on screen can be identified from the studies as common criteria in viewers' judgements of violence. The main criteria are as follows:

Closeness
The more distance, in terms of geography, time and other relationships, between the violence and the viewer, the less disturbing they will find it. This principle is evident in studies of viewers' reactions to both factual and fictional violence.

Status
Viewers' identification with victims and perpetrators of violence is seen to influence their perceptions of violence in both factual and fictional programmes. Violence inflicted on innocent victims is more distressing to viewers than violence suffered by a guilty victim.

Certainty
Studies relating mainly to factual programmes found that viewers are less disturbed and concerned by violence in cases where they fully understand the situation in which it occurred and know the outcome of the violence.

Minimalism
This is applicable to factual programmes, and in particular to news. Viewers are concerned that violent imagery should not be used in greater detail than is necessary to illustrate the point being made.

Realism
In general, the research showed that realistic violence disturbs viewers more than unrealistic or fantasy violence. Thus, viewers are more concerned by violence in factual programmes than in fictional programmes. Furthermore, within the fictional genre, viewers are disturbed more by realistic violence such as that in Crime Dramas than that which they see as unrealistic.

Other factors found to influence viewers' perceptions of violence on television relate directly to the characteristics of the viewer. The studies clearly show that viewers' interpretations of violence are differentiated by age, sex, personal levels of aggression and personal experience of violence. The studies relating to the way children perceive violence show that children's perceptions do not differ significantly from adults' perceptions. Indeed, the research indicates that even very young children are able to distinguish between various forms of violence. Children also employ various coping strategies to handle the emotions that they experience when watching violence on television.

The findings illustrate that viewers' fear of real life violence is, in certain cases, influenced by screen violence. Heavy exposure to violence and crime on television can cause some people to exaggerate the dangers of everyday life. Research reviewed in this chapter also reveals that, in addition to the possible negative effects of watching violence on television, the possible effects of violence in video games also concern the public.

The research reviewed makes it clear that it would be wrong to treat the audience as passive viewers in the way that studies of media effects of violence have often tended to do. The research clearly illustrates that viewers watch media violence in an active and involved way. Viewers interpret a range of contextual factors as outlined above in order to discern between various types of violence presented by the media, and from these they then construct judgements of the violence shown. The studies in chapter five also provide an insight into the implications of the sociological background of viewers on perceptions of televised violence. For instance, previous experience of violence, gender, and particularities of lifestyle – such as living on one's own – contribute to the ways in which viewers perceive violence. By taking these factors into account, such studies locate the viewer as a person, and explore the possible explanations for the different meanings that viewers attribute to violence on television. Therefore, the study of audience perceptions of violence plays an important role in the ongoing development of our understanding of mediated experiences. However, more often than not, the motivation for funding audience perceptions research is founded on the strength of public concern over the possible negative effects of televised violence in society. As already discussed in the introduction, the political origins of many of the organisations that fund research into audience perceptions of violence come from a need to address this public concern. Whilst the studies of audience perceptions of violence are related to some extent to concerns over the possible effects of television, they nevertheless have a significant independent value in terms of understanding how the audience processes screen violence, and in doing so, makes judgements about what they see.

Bibliography

Anderson, C. A. & Dill, K. E. (2000) 'Video Games and Aggressive Thoughts, Feelings, and Behavior in the Laboratory and in Life', *Journal Of Personality And Social Psychology*, Vol 78; Part 4: 772-790.

American Psychological Association (A.P.A) Commission On Youth & Violence.

Australian Broadcasting Authority (1994) *'Cool' or 'gross': Children's attitudes to violence, kissing, and swearing on television* Monograph 4.

Australian Broadcasting Authority (1996) *Your Say: A Review of audience concerns about Australia's broadcast media 1996.*

Australian Broadcasting Authority (2000) *Children and media harm* Monograph 10.

Australian Broadcasting Authority and the Office of Film and Literature Classification (1993) *Classification Issues: Film, Video & Television.*

Australian Broadcasting Tribunal (1990) *Television Violence in Australia: Report to the Minister for Transport and Communications.* Sydney: Commonwealth of Australia.

Australian Broadcasting Tribunal (1991) *Sex, Violence and Offensive Language: Community Views on Classification of Television Programmes*, Monograph 2.

Barlow, G and Hill, A. (1985) *Video Violence and Children* London : Hodder and Stoughton.

British Broadcasting Corporation (1993) *Guidelines for the Portrayal of Violence on Television.*

Broadcasting Standards Council (1996) Research Working Paper, 13 *Young People and the Media* – report on teenagers by Andrea Millwood Hargrave and Report on Television in the Family by Professor James D. Halloran and Peggy Gray.

Broadcasting Standards Commission (1997) *Monitoring Report 5:* 1996.

Broadcasting Standards Commission (1998) *Monitoring Report 6:* 1997.

Broadcasting Standards Commission (1999) *Monitoring Report 7:* 1998.

Broadcasting Standards Commission (2000) Briefing update No6: *Matters of Offence.*

Broadcasting Standards Commission (2000a) Briefing Update No.5. *Regulation – The Changing Perspective.*

Bryant, Jennings & Zillmann, Dolf (1991) *Responding to the screen: reception and reaction processes*, Hillsdale, N.J. and London: Erlbaum.

Buckingham, D (1996) *Understanding Children's Emotional Responses To Television*, Manchester: Manchester University Press.

Cantor, J (1994). 'Fright reactions to mass media'. In Bryant, J. and Zillmann, D. (Eds), *Media Effects*, Hillsdale, NJ: Erlbaum.

Cumberbatch, G and Howitt, D (1989) *A Measure of Uncertainty: The Effects of the Mass Media*, Broadcasting Standards Council Research Monograph Series 1, London: John Libbey.

Cumberbatch, G (2000) Only a game?, *New Scientist*, 10 June 2000. pp 44-45.

Docherty, D (1990) Broadcasting Standards Council Annual Review 1990, *Violence in Television Fiction*, London: John Libbey.

Doob, A.N. & Macdonald, C.E (1979) 'Television viewing and fear of victimization: Is the relationship causal?', *Journal of Personality and Social Psychology* Vol.37: 170-179.

Freedman, N (1984) 'Effects of Television on Aggression', *Psychology Bulletin* 96 (2): 227-246.

Gauntlett, D (1995) *Moving Experiences: Understanding Televisions Influences and Effects*, Academia Research Monograph, 13. London: John Libbey.

Geertz, Clifford (1993) *The Interpretation of Cultures: Selected Essays*, London: Fontana Press.

Gerbner, G & Gross, L (1976) 'Living with television: The violence profile', *Journal of Communications* Vol.26: 173-199.

Gerbner, G., Gross, L., Jackson-Beeck,M. Jeffries-Fox, S. and Signorielli, N. (1978) 'Cultural indicators: violence profile no.9', *Journal of Communication*, *28*, 176-207.

Gerbner, G., Gross, L., Signorielli, N., Morgan, M., and Jackson-Beeck,M. (1979) *The demonstration of power: violence profile no.10*, *Journal of Communication*, *28*, 177-196.

Goldstein, J.H (1994) *Toys, Play and Child Development*, Cambridge [England] New York: Cambridge University Press.

Greenfield, P.M (1984) *Mind and Media – The Effects of Television, Video Games and Computers*, London: Fontana Paperbacks.

Griffiths, Mark (1999) 'Video Games and Aggression: A Review of the Literature', *Aggression and Violent Behavior*, Vol 4, No.2, pp 203-212.

Gulbenkian Foundation (1995) *Children and Violence; Report of the Commission On Children and Violence*, London: Calouste Gulbenkian Foundation.

Gunter, B (1979) 'Television Violence and Entertainment Value', *The Bulletin of The British Psychological Society* March, 1979. Vol.32: pp 100-103.

Gunter, B (1985) *Dimensions of Violence*, Aldershot: Gower.

Gunter, B (1987) *Television and the Fear of Crime*, Independent Broadcasting Authority Television Research Monograph. London: John Libbey.

Gunter, B (1988) 'The Importance of Studying Viewers' Perceptions of Violence on Television', *Current Psychology* Vol.7, No.1:26-43.

Gunter, B, Sancho-Aldridge, J & Winstone, P (1994) *Television: The Public's View 1993* (Independent Television Commission Research Monograph Series) London: John Libbey.

Gunter, B & Furnham, A (1984) 'Perceptions of television violence: Effects of programmes genre and the physical form of violence', *British Journal Of Social Psychology* Vol.23: 155-184.

Gunter, B & McLaughlin, C (1992) *Television: The Public's View*, (Independent Television Commission Research Monograph Series) London: John Libbey.

Gunter, B & Winstone, P. (1993) *Television: The Public's View 1992*, (Independent Television Commission Research Monograph Series) London: John Libbey.

Gunter, B and Wober, M (1988) *Violence on Television: What the Viewers Think*, Independent Broadcasting Authority, London: John Libbey.

Halloran, James.D and Gray, Peggy (1996) 'Television in The Family' in Broadcasting Standards Council (1996) Research Working Paper, 13 *Young People and the Media*.

Hoffner, Cynthia *et al.* (2001) 'The Third Person Effect in Perceptions of the Influence of Television Violence', *Journal of Communication*, Vol. 51: pp 283-299.

Home Office Standing Conference on Crime Prevention (1989) '*Report of the Working Group on the Fear of Crime*', 11 December, 1989.

Howitt, D & Cumberbatch, G (1974) 'Audience perceptions of violent television content', *Communications Research* (1): pp 204-223.

Independent Television Commission (1995) *Television: The Public's View: 1994*, (ITC Research Publication) London: John Libbey.

Independent Television Commission (1996) *Television: The Public's View: 1995*, (ITC Research Publication) London: John Libbey.

Independent Television Commission (1997) *Television: The Public's View: 1996*, (ITC Research Publication) London: John Libbey.

Independent Television Commission (1998) *Television: The Public's View: 1997*, (ITC Research Publication) Luton: University of Luton Press.

Independent Television Commission (2000) *Television: The Public's View: 2000*, (ITC Research Publication).

Independent Television Commission (2001) *Television: The Public's View: 2001*, (ITC Research Publication).

Kieran, M, Morrison, D.E and Svennevig, M (2000) 'Privacy, the public and journalism: towards an analytic framework', *Journalism*, Vol.1(2):145-169.

Kindler (1991) in Strasburger, V.C (1995) *Adolescents and the Media – Medical and Psychological Impact*, London: Sage publications.

Krcmar, M. and Cooke, M. (2001) Children's Moral reasoning and Their Perceptions of Television Violence, *Journal of Communication*, Vol51: 300-316.

Lagerspetz, KMJ, Wahlroos, C and Wendelin, C (1978) 'Facial expressions of pre -school children while watching televised violence', *Scandinavian Journal of Psychology*, Vol.19: 213-222.

Livingstone, Sonia (1990) *Making Senses of Television: The psychology of audience interpretation*', London:Routledge.

Livingstone, Sonia & Bovill, Moira (1999) *'Young People New Media'* Report of the Research Project 'Children, Young People and the Changing Media Environment'.

Mehrabian, A & Wixen, W.J (1986) 'Preferences for Individual Video Games as a function of their emotional effects on players' *Journal of Applied Psychology* Vol. 16: 3-15.

Millwood Hargrave, A (ed.) (1993) *Violence in Factual Television*, London: John Libbey.

Morrison, D.E (1992) *Television and the Gulf War*, Academia Research Monograph 7, London: John Libbey.

Morrison, D.E (1999) *Defining Violence: The Search for Understanding*, Luton: University of Luton Press.

Morrison, D.E (2000) *'The Search for an Understanding: Administrative Communications Research and Focus Group in Practice'*, Luton: University of Luton Press.

Morrison, D.E and MacGregor, B (1993) 'Detailed Findings from Editing Groups', in Millwood Hargrave, A (ed.), (1993) *Violence in Factual Television*, London: John Libbey.

Morrison, D.E & MacGregor, B (1995) 'From focus groups to editing groups: a new method of reception analysis', *Media, Culture & Society* Vol. 17: 141-150.

Morrison, D.E and Svennevig, M (2002) *The Public Interest, the Media and Privacy*, A report for British Broadcasting Corporation, Broadcasting Standards Commission, Independent Committee for the Supervision of Standards of

Telephone Information Services, Independent Television Commission, Institute for Public Policy Research, The Radio Authority.

National Television Violence Study, Volume 1, 1994-95, (1996) Thousand Oaks, CA: Sage Publications.

National Television Violence Study, Volume 2, 1995-96 (1997) Thousand Oaks, CA: Sage Publications.

National Television Violence Study, Volume 3, 1996-97 (1998) Thousand Oaks, CA: Sage Publications.

Parke, R.D., Berkowitz, L., Leyens, J.P., West, S.G., and Sebastian, R.J. (1977) 'Some effects of violent and non-violent movies on the behaviour of juvenile delinquents', in Berkowitz, L (ed.), *Advance in Experimental Psychology*, Vol.10. New York: Academic Press.

Potter, W. James (1999) *On Media Violence* Thousand Oaks, CA: Sage.

Provenzo, Eugene F (1991) *Video Kids: Making Sense of Nintendo*, Cambridge, MA: Harvard University Press.

Redfern, S (1988) *Violence and the Media*, London: BBC.

Schlesinger, P, Dobash, R.E, Dobash, R.P, and Weaver, C.K (1992) *Women Viewing Violence*, London: British Film Institute.

Schlesinger, P, Haynes, R, Boyles, R, McNair, B, Dobash, R.E, & Dobash, R.P (1998) *Men Viewing Violence*, London: Broadcasting Standards Commission.

Shaw, M and Carr-Hill, R (1991) *Public Opinion, Media and Violence – Attitudes to the Gulf War in a Local Population*, Hull: University of Hull.

Shearer, A (1991) *Survivors and the Media*, Broadcasting Standards Council Research Monograph Series 2, London: John Libbey.

Silvern, S, Willhamson, P, & Countermine, T (1983) 'Video Game Playing and Aggression in Young Children', Paper presented to the American Education Research Association.

Snow, R.P (1974) 'How Children Interpret Television Violence in Play Context', *Journalism Quarterly* 51: 13-21.

Strasburger, V.C (1995) *Adolescents and the Media – Medical and Psychological Impact*, London: Sage.

Svennevig, M (1998) *Television Across The Years: The British Public's View*, Luton: University of Luton Press.

Van der Voort, T.H.A (1986) *Television violence: A Child's Eye View*, Amsterdam, Holland: Elsevier Science Publishers.

Verhulst, Stefaan (2001) '*Reflecting Community Values: Public Attitudes to Broadcasting Regulation*' Broadcasting Standards Commission.

Video Standards Council – discussion with Dr Guy Cumberbatch – http://www.videostandards.org.uk/video_violence.htm.

Wober, M & Gunter, B (1982) 'Television and Personal Threat – Fact or artefact – A British Survey', *British Journal of Psychology* Vol. 21. Sep: 239-247.

Coping with a Relative's Addiction

Advice for handling addictive
behaviours in family situations

Northlands Centre

VERITAS

Published 2010 by Veritas Publications
7–8 Lower Abbey Street
Dublin 1
Ireland

Reprinted 2011

publications@veritas.ie · www.veritas.ie

ISBN 978 1 84730 248 9

10 9 8 7 6 5 4 3 2

Designed by Tanya M. Ross, Veritas
Printed in Ireland by Hudson Killeen, Dublin

Veritas books are printed on paper made from the wood pulp of
managed forests. For every tree felled, at least one tree is planted,
thereby renewing natural resources.

Acknowledgements

This book is informed by all those who have brought their struggle with addiction to Northlands. Your courage in what you have shared, whether the addiction was yours or that of someone close to you, is the enduring foundation of what follows. Despite the painful journeys taken by so many, the legacy of all these encounters is the hope and belief that recovery can happen for all concerned. It is inspiring and privileged work.

Our sincere thanks are due to all the staff and volunteers at Northlands who contributed their experience with such openness and generosity. They provided the humanity and depth that has enriched this exploration of a difficult and complex subject.

Our thanks also go to Donna Doherty of Veritas for her guidance and encouragement through the stages of this endeavour.

Christina McClements
Mary Wilson

COPING WITH A RELATIVE'S ADDICTION

Contents

Introduction

This book is written for anyone who is suffering from the effects of addictive behaviours. The situation you find yourself in is likely to be chaotic, painful and seemingly hopeless.

The purpose of these chapters is to untangle the confusion that accompanies dependency, to explain its progression, and to set out the behaviours that allow it to continue. Crucially, this book offers an understanding of the exhaustion, frustration and fears that set in among family members. It explores the coping methods (helpful and not-so-helpful) often adopted by those concerned.

Addiction protects itself. It generates great selfishness and causes a great deal of hurt. The symptoms of addiction (mental, physical, emotional and spiritual) are not confined to the person who is using, drinking, over-medicating or gambling. They infect every aspect of that person's relationships, damaging those in close contact and disturbing the dynamic of the family involved. Likewise the recovery process is not just the privilege of the addicted person. Those close to them also deserve support in their own recovery, whether or not their loved one achieves sobriety or abstinence.

We acknowledge that addiction takes many different forms: gambling, eating disorders, self-harming, Internet and sexual. While the compulsion behind all these behaviours has common characteristics, the emphasis of this book is on dependency to chemical substances. As alcohol is the primary addiction in Irish society, there is certainly a focus on this in the case studies. Illegal drugs and medications are problematic throughout our society and these also have been given substantial attention.

The subject of the book, however, is the individual rather than the substance. It is not a book that offers a scientific analysis of addictive substances; rather it displays the unfolding of the very human deterioration that occurs at a deeply personal level to the user and to those who live with them as dependency takes hold. It also sets out the pathways to achieving recovery. There is no set formula for every family, and this book takes account of the different backgrounds and values that are variously held in our society.

The book first sets out the characteristics and progression of addiction. Following on from this we look at real-life scenarios.

Throughout the book the terms 'addiction' and 'dependency' are used interchangeably: physical and psychological addiction are profoundly entwined and are not experienced as distinct conditions. Also, we will refer to 'use' and 'user' in relation to both alcohol and drugs.

It is intended that this book offer clarity, guidance and hope to those who are left feeling isolated and helpless by another's addiction. Above all, it is hoped that those affected will be encouraged to reach out for further support. Recovery is possible – for everyone concerned.

1. Problem, Habit, or Addiction?

....

I find it astounding now that it took me fifteen years to understand that addiction was the problem. The realisation of this was so gradual and slow. Mark was not ticking all the boxes that amounted to 'alcoholic' as I understood it. I wish I had listened more to my own instinct. (Greta)

I questioned everything about my ability as a mother. I wondered if I should have left my husband. I even blamed myself for marrying an alcoholic in case this had been the start of her problem. (Jean)

I thought that if I behaved better, then Mammy might not drink as much. I tried so hard to make her stop. (Maria)

Am I over-reacting?

It is often difficult to be certain about where responsibility for addiction lies. It is difficult to discern truth from exaggeration. We can feel very unsure, and doubt our ability to judge the situation. Where there is addiction there is always confusion: 'Am I over-reacting?'

This chapter sets out to clear up the confusion. In order for you as a relative to understand what has happened to a loved one, we would ask you to bear with us in looking at addiction itself. Perhaps the thing that causes greatest suffering for families is the lack of clarity around the condition. Indeed, this is often what allows it to continue. The shifts from recreational to problematic to dependent use are subtle. It is useful to look at each pattern of use and examine how a person moves from occasional harmless drinking or drug use to the phase of full-blown addiction. What follows is a breakdown of the addictive process right from its earliest stages.

The four routes to addiction

1. The gradual, social route
This is how many people learn to manage their substance use. Generally this begins as a pleasurable style of use in social situations, and does not evolve into problem behaviours for the majority of people. However, if social use over the years becomes heavy and frequent, the risk of addiction increases.

2. Heavy drinking/drug use from the start
The 'going out to get blocked' or 'out of your head' is a common approach in our culture, especially at weekends. This bingeing then leaves us more open to the possibility of mixing substances, which in turn leads to the heightened risk of accidents or overdose, or at the very least, embarrassing and uncomfortable memories of the night before.

3. Heavy use from the start to escape circumstances
Examples of these circumstances are unemployment, poverty and family conflict. Heavy substance use on top of a difficult or unstable situation does not help our ability to deal with it. It also gives us the illusion that our intoxication is the safest and most comfortable place to be, far removed from a harsh reality. The appeal is obvious and dependency can set in quickly through this route.

4. Heavy use to escape internal unease
Such use is a deliberate tactic to ease emotional – or physical – pain. We seek the distraction and the numbing effect of the substance. Oblivion is an easier place to be for us. In using it to avoid the source of our pain, we quickly lose touch with the reality around us and the feelings within us.

Even these distinct roads to dependency can become merged: someone who uses or drinks occasionally and within limits can turn to alcohol or drug-induced numbness after trauma or loss. Using or drinking in relation to the third point above – to escape the circumstances around us – can then often lead to medicating the painful emotions that such circumstances give rise to, in turn leading to the fourth point of escaping internal unease. The patterns of drinking or using, then, can quickly become more harmful when life becomes difficult.

It must be remembered that individuals slide into dependent use at different rates. Furthermore, the effects of addiction to drugs such as cocaine and heroin become more apparent at an earlier stage. For the purpose of clarity, we will examine the process of dependency by looking at the social route of addiction – where dependency and addiction is built up over time – from the initial, vague hints of trouble to the devastation of the later stages.

The stages of addiction

The social route to dependency has pleasurable beginnings. Many people find that certain drugs such as alcohol and cannabis reduce shyness and self-consciousness; they ease the way into social situations and help us to relax. Other substances such as speed and cocaine provide us with a rush of endorphin hormones, boosting the sense of self-confidence and energy. With inhibitions dulled, even the introvert can be expressive, witty and outgoing. They no longer have to be on guard about what to say or how to say it.

At this stage there is little price to pay. If the intake is excessive there may be a few hangovers or comedowns, or some over-spending; indeed there may be a few embarrassments, but this is outweighed by the sense of an evening well spent.

The important aspect of this is the learning around the perceived positive effects of the substances. The feelings that they give are warm and comfortable. Drinkers/users have found a way to change moods, ease discomfort and distract from everyday concerns. They can 'get a high' and return to a normal state of feeling when the evening has passed. In their view there are no serious consequences for them or those around them, and any damage done can usually be rectified or healed. It is still worth it. For many people this becomes their style of drinking. It remains social, occasional and generally within healthy limits.

The early stage of addiction

Now there is a subtle shift away from occasional use of the substance to a relationship being built up with the substance – it has become like a friend who can be trusted to lift the mood. Users knows that it will work, and gradually can come to see the drink or drug not just as a means to heighten the feeling of a good night, but to actively avoid uncomfortable feelings or moods. Using or drinking to relieve an emotion is a huge warning sign, and one that is often missed.

Now the use is more frequent. The body has learnt to tolerate the effects of the substance and it takes more to achieve the desired result. Increased use leads to increased need. While the ability to cope with the substance increases, the ability to cope with the demands of everyday living decreases. This is not just because more intensive use leaves the drinkers and users rather fragile at times, physically and emotionally; now they have found a quick fix, a short cut through discomfort. There is no patience anymore for the minor irritations, which are felt more quickly and more keenly.

The user becomes less patient, more irritable and more sensitised to criticism. Their edginess and frustration confuses those around them. Misunderstandings, atmospheres and arguments then happen. They become more defensive. They are hurt more readily. Their feelings are often uncomfortable. But they can find relief. They plan and anticipate the next session of drinking or drug use. They turn to the substance that they know will relieve these feelings.

Here the cause and the cure have been confused: the user has inadvertently turned to a substance to cure the difficulties it has caused. It is this belief that will drag people further into problematic use.

There is now a cost to those around the person using. Their short temper can be hard to live with. But now the user blames those who so easily provoke it. They believe that the problems are around them rather than within them, and they do not recognise the change occurring in their personalities. Those around them, however, feel it deeply and are confused by it. Already faced with irritability, the family wonders if they might be to blame. Then they may wonder about the drinking or drug use. There is no clarity about the amounts being taken, and questioning will likely be met with a defensive response.

The 'social route' sees a gradual build-up of using over time. There have been good times and happy memories. But now things are turning rather sour. There are more hangovers and worse comedowns. As drink or drugs move up the scale of personal priorities, users become more defensive about the substance and more rigid in their need for it. They are frustrated by anything and anyone who threatens to interfere with their pattern of use. They are more easily stressed and less able to cope with difficult days than they used to be. They feel less euphoric on the chosen substance and less comfortable without it. They deflect the discomfort onto those closest to them.

There are signs of trouble at this stage that can be missed by the users: they do not see that the substance use is the cause of difficulties. The family may be more suspicious that the use is a factor, but in the face of defensiveness they may doubt their judgement.

This is a very important stage: if the drinker or user realises and acknowledges what is happening, it is possible to undo the pattern of growing dependency. It needs a serious change in thinking and lifestyle, but it can be done. If this realisation is denied, they will continue to justify the behaviour.

The family is also feeling vulnerable. They are aware of increasing substance use. They grow concerned: the user does not. They are told they are over-reacting; everything and everyone gets blamed except for the substance being used. There are always excuses. The self-doubt begins to set in. Have the family got it wrong? Are they over-reacting? Is this just a phase that their loved one will soon let go? For some people it may be a phase. But others will progress on their path to dependency.

The middle stage of addiction

Here, at some level, the person who is drinking or using knows that it is causing problems. Facing this reality, though, would demand that they do something about it, and this feels like too high an expectation. They believe that they cannot cope without this substance. Indeed, their ability to cope has been seriously weakened in the course of heavy use. It is easier to keep using or drinking than to stop.

And so they protect themselves from this demand. They avoid the people who might question their drinking/using behaviour and the places where it might be noticed. They may even avoid events where their chemical needs cannot be met. As with all pastimes, they seek the company of people who use or drink as they do. This may not be a conscious choice but it allows them to believe that there is nothing abnormal or extreme about their own habits. There is always someone who takes more than they do. They may also be self-medicating hangovers, withdrawals or comedowns with other drugs.

Lives and relationships are becoming disrupted. The user has become unable to separate issues or see their substance use clearly. Automatically they blame circumstances or other people. They are convinced that if all the other problems were removed, resolved or changed, there would be no problem with substance use. The substance, they believe, helps them cope with it all. And so they continue to seek solace in the very thing that is the cause of the disruption.

They are in a personal battle of control. They try to prove to themselves and others that they can choose the level of their use. There is a strong need to believe that they can still use socially and recreationally. They may only smoke joints before bedtime; they only take a few lines of coke at parties on the weekend; they give up spirits and stick with beer; they give up the drink for Lent. There are promises that the use has changed. Repeatedly promises are broken and remorse, although at times heartfelt, is short-lived. Inevitably they fall back into a pattern of excessive use very quickly.

They might change pubs, dealers, jobs, accommodation, towns, company – but the patterns of using ultimately stay the same. They run into a cycle of frustration and despair. And still they use.

There are contradictions now between values and actions, a failure to treat people with the care and respect they used to treat them with. They lie, neglect the family, and are offensive to the people closest to them. Alcohol or drugs have dulled inhibitions, judgement and conscience. Despite the need to believe that this is not their fault and that it has nothing to do with the substance use, there is a deeply disturbing underlying feeling present. But now they know how to deaden these feelings, and so they continue to use.

There are no more highs now – they are not happy with it and not happy without it. They are constantly in a place of emotional discomfort which using only partly relieves. They are totally preoccupied with getting supplies of the substance at the cost of the usual daily concerns.

Serious physical and emotional problems plague the user. They may have stomach ulcers, accidental injuries, loss of concentration and short-term memory. They are defensive, secretive, deceitful, bad-tempered and unpredictable. They lose interest in their appearance and health. They do not eat well. Yet they cannot see how ill they are, or how unacceptably they are behaving. The damage is obvious to everyone but themselves.

They have lost any control over their use, and they have lost touch with reality. They have also lost control over their lives. This damage is progressive. If they do not seek help at this point, then recovery will be more difficult to attain.

The family is also deeply troubled by this stage. They have no doubt now that the drinking or drug use is a serious problem. Family members are exhausted trying to challenge the behaviour and to emotionally survive the destruction that goes with it. At this stage it is often these family members who are the ones to seek support. Recovery frequently starts with them.

The late stage of addiction

Now users' lives are coming apart. They are in a state of chronic chaos. They are both physically and mentally ill with their addiction. They get drunk or stoned quickly on much smaller amounts. The damage done to the liver and brain means that they are unable to cope with the effects of the drug, to break down the chemical or to withstand the effects.

They are constantly in the zone of emotional pain: drinking or using is an attempt to feel normal. They face hellish three-day comedowns or hangovers. They emerge from blackouts with shakes and horrors. They experience distorted thinking and extreme emotional distress, sometimes involving suicidal thoughts or attempts. Depression and despair are constant and they can no longer escape the guilt, shame and hopelessness. But still they try. The substance is the only crutch left and they cling to it.

All normality is gone, whether they are sober or using, in their lives and in their family's lives. If they cannot find a way to stop using now, it is likely that their addiction will kill them.

At this stage the family – if they still have a relationship with the addicted person – can do little more than provide nursing care to someone who is now physically and mentally sick. If it gets to this, the family members can lose sight of their own need for care and support. Emotionally they have little left to give, but can be trapped in the role of caregiver as the addicted person becomes more chronically ill.

2. The Feelings Disorder

There is a feelings dimension to every human life. We react with our feelings to events, situations and other people. Feelings can be positive: we can be joyful, relieved, hopeful, affirmed. Feelings can also be uncomfortable: we can be distressed, hurt, resentful, jealous, ashamed, grief-stricken. Our memories and experiences are rooted in our feelings.

Our feelings can shift and fade over hours and minutes. Or they can be so persistent that they set the tone and quality of our lives. They can give enormous and deep satisfaction. They can also cause such huge distress that our physical health is impacted.

Emotional awareness is central to our well-being. It is through the recognition and expression of our feelings that we can gauge how we are doing in relation to other people and in the world, and process what is happening in our lives. Feelings allow us to be connected to each other at a deeper level. When we share our joys, fears and vulnerabilities, we allow another to understand how we experience the world – we bring that person closer to us.

Feelings are what make us human; they are natural and healthy – the good and the bad. They are sensors that alert us to the helpful and the harmful in our environment. In this way our feelings can be very accurate even when our thinking isn't straight. However, at other times they can be so strong that they cloud and distort our judgement. If we suffer bereavement we grieve. This is painful. But in feeling this pain and in expressing it we are dealing with the loss. Only in allowing ourselves to experience our feelings and working through them can we really heal and move forward. Otherwise our feelings get stuck. They fester if not dealt with. We become emotionally unwell.

Circumstances of individual lives vary and some people are subject to more emotional hardship and distress than others. Some are overloaded at an early age. Instinctively we prefer to avoid painful and uncomfortable feelings. We all develop a range of defensive strategies that help us achieve this to various extents. Some of us turn to chemicals or behaviours that can distract us from or distort these feelings in a way that becomes dangerously unhealthy for us.

Feelings, alcohol and drugs

Alcohol, cannabis, cocaine, tranquillisers and all illicit or illegal drugs are mood-altering chemicals. Depressant drugs, such as alcohol and cannabis, act much as an anaesthetic. They shut down physical and emotional pain. Stimulants such as cocaine and speed raise the hormone levels, creating a buzz of confidence and excitement. They change our mood by chemical reaction, disrupting the natural hormonal balance in the brain. Feelings are dulled, heightened or distorted. We enter a false reality of artificial emotion based on chemical manipulation as opposed to what is really happening around us and within us.

This is an exaggerated version of what happens naturally at times of emotional reaction. If joyful or exciting events happen to us, our brains respond by releasing serotonin and dopamine. At a physiological level this is how we experience feelings of happiness and joy. In times of stress or grief our brains release adrenalin and cortisol, crucial in the 'fight or flight' response. The brain is the largest producer of drugs in their pure form, usually appropriate to the circumstances in our lives. This is an accurate response to the events we experience.

Association between heightened mood and the drug of choice gathers momentum. The drug of choice and the good feelings become inseparable. Both the drug and the escapist behaviour can become a habit. Regular and heavy use of mood-altering chemical substances inevitably results in physiological and emotional consequences. Repeatedly assaulted by mood-altering chemicals, the brain becomes less effective at producing its own appropriate doses. The user's emotions become flat and dulled, especially when stimulants are the drug of choice. Due to a loss in the brain's natural regulation, the moods can fluctuate to extremes. Repressed feelings threaten to explode; frustration and confusion cause the user to retreat from or assail those around them. There is an urgent desire to avoid the low moods that come as part of common boredom or dissatisfaction and to experience the buzz that is associated with the substance. The buzz, though, is more a memory than an achievable reality now. More of the drug is used, and used more often. More time, energy and money are spent chasing the elusive feel-good factor.

Ironically it is the reverse that happens: the repression and avoidance of real feeling leads inevitably towards depression. Users/drinkers hover on the brink of confused emotions, unable to understand what is happening to them. They get busy chasing the substance and avoiding the consequences in them and around them. Despair deepens but cannot be faced. When it is not faced it cannot be dealt with. The confidence needed to deal with people and with everyday irritations is eroded. Problems gather up and the task of dealing with them seems too big. Avoidance, drinking and using deepen. Such avoidance deepens emotional damage and blocks the opportunity to heal. Healing can be a painful process. We would not amputate a broken limb to avoid the pain of its repair, yet we so easily cut off the range of the feelings we should experience in the hope that we can take a short-cut to happiness.

The dream promised by the drug turns to a nightmare. The user has not gained popularity, confidence, coping skills or happiness. They are increasingly isolated, frightened, angry and depressed. The feelings they have suppressed are buried alive within them, and harden into rigid attitudes. Repressing any aspect of the self increases its power – it will find expression, however skewed. The feelings of resentment, anger, arrogance and self-pity become part of the personality. Dependent drinkers and users can become arrogant, angry, resentful and self-pitying people. This is part of their defensiveness. But there are deeper feelings that feed this – the user is afraid, hurt and ashamed. Until there is an awareness and an acceptance of these feelings they cannot be faced or understood. Nothing can change. They are trapped in emotional pain, distressed when not using and often distressed too in the act of using. The feeling of euphoria is a distant memory: the substance is used in a desperate search for normality. But there is no normality now. The vague sense of hurt and despair deepens and becomes all-absorbing and ever-present. But the belief that there is relief in the substance is entrenched, despite the evidence that it is making everything more intolerable.

Physically, most substances do bring relief in the short-term. There is a cycle of drinking or using until the sickness is so great that continuing is not an option. Then the alcoholic faces the shakes and the retching. The drug user is assaulted by anxiety, muscle spasms and a digestive meltdown. All are battered by an emotional aftermath of guilt, panic and personal failure. In the cold light of day the mess cannot be avoided – yet neither can it be managed. The chaos is too great. The drugs have wiped out the physical and mental resources to cope with anything. This is the trap of full-blown, self-destructive addiction. It is why alcoholics represent one of the largest identifiable groups of those who attempt suicide.

Delusion, confusion and denial

Delusion is a form of distorted thinking where the ability to see reality with accuracy is lost. Repeated use of mood-altering substances has misled the mind. Reality, as perceived by the addicted drinker or user, is that alcohol or drugs bring relief and make circumstances more tolerable – despite a wealth of evidence to the contrary. In fact alcohol has resulted in repeated disaster and eroded any ability to cope. The need to believe that alcohol is helpful and rewarding is deeply embedded; challenging this belief threatens the only coping strategy left to the drinker – reliance on alcohol. As long as the drinker or user does not see the horror of their situation, then they do not see the necessity to change it.

This is extremely frustrating for those around the person who is in trouble, for they have little defence against the consequences of addicted use. The continued destruction and self-destruction makes no sense to observers who find it hard to understand why it should not simply stop. They wonder why and how their loved one keeps inflicting suffering on themselves and those around them. The addicted person does so because they are addicted, and they continue to be with the help of a range of unconscious defence mechanisms that help them. When someone has lost trust, relationships, job and health because of their substance use, and they alone do not see the substance as the problem, they are suffering from delusion. There are subtle ways in which the mind allows this to develop, and the most obvious of them is denial.

What is denial?

Denial is one of many defence mechanisms that we are all capable of using in daily life when a situation becomes too uncomfortable to deal with. There is a range of these protections and they can be gathered under the title of denial. The glaring feature of addiction is the constant insistence that there is no problem. It is difficult to believe that the person cannot see the problem. Denial can take many forms, and the main ones are set out below.

Simple denial: The drinker/user has convinced themselves that 'Everything is okay – there's no problem and there's no reason for me to think that there's anything wrong or unusual about my drinking or drug use. I'm coping with both my situation and my feelings. Nothing's wrong with me.'

There are other features of denial that reinforce this wild distortion of reality:

Minimising: An acknowledgement and admission that the use carries some level of problem, but in such a way that it is presented as much less serious or significant than it is in reality. 'I'm a bit heavy on it at times/I'm a bit fond of the jar, but I don't drink as much as my mates. It's not that bad.'

Repression: An unconscious mechanism to divert us from dwelling on the embarrassing elements of our behaviour, the extent of the drinking or using, and the consequences to others and to our own values system. We shift uncomfortable truths to the back of our minds: 'I wouldn't do that.'

Euphoric recall: A recollection of 'the good old days' when drinking or drug use was fun, sociable and associated with youth, friendship and even romance. While the reality of current drinking and use is more about embarrassment, despair and regret, the user/drinker will cling to the nostalgia of happy times and hope that they can rediscover these feelings through their use. Without realising that the good times have gone sour, the dependent person chases the hope, based on selective memory, that these are still 'the good times in my life'.

Blaming and projection: The shifting of responsibility for our behaviour onto someone or something else as a way of rationalising the using behaviour and explaining the problem. 'It's the boss/the wife/the kids/the recession/my depression ... Is it any wonder I drink!'

Rationalising: The litany of reasons, excuses and justifications that keep us well removed from our feelings. Here the drinking or use is not denied, but it is explained as a consequence to events outside us rather than on the addiction within us. 'When I get through this bad patch I'll be fine.'

Intellectualising: Resituating the problem from the personal to the theoretical. This claim to knowledge and academic understanding outwits the complainant and places the drinker/user in a self-perceived position of superiority. It also provides another layer of armour to distance the user from their feelings. 'I've read the books on psychology – I know what this is about and what needs to be done to sort it out.'

Diversion: Blatant changing of the subject, whether it is the global economy, climate change, or the failings of a mutual acquaintance: 'There are worse problems than my smoking/drinking/gambling – lets talk about something else.'

Self-pity: A deeply felt and long-nurtured feeling of hurt and persecution, the belief that the drinker has suffered to an intolerable degree, and that this is eased rather than intensified by chemicals: 'You wouldn't understand.'

Hostility: A tactic to ensure that observers learn very quickly that any reference or threat to the addictive behaviour will result in their feeling unsettled, hurt or embarrassed: 'This topic is out of bounds. Back off – or else!'

Blackouts

While not strictly a defence mechanism, blackouts do protect the drinker from seeing the reality of their drinking. 'Blackout' in this context does not mean passing out. It is specific to heavy alcohol use and is one of the first warning signs that can tell the drinker that they are crossing into dangerous levels of use.

A blackout can only be realised after the event. Because the drinker was conscious and functioning in a way that seemed quite normal to all around them, it can come as a surprise to the drinker and those who were with them to realise that they have no recollection at all of parts of the evening. The ironic feature of a blackout is that the drinker does not appear to be incapably drunk. Blackouts vary in their intensity and duration. Generally, the more serious the drink problem, the longer the time-span that is lost.

Every forgotten drink-fuelled incident builds on the hurt, distrust and contempt felt by family members. They can be left with the memory of embarrassing behaviour, of promises fervently made, or of hurtful remarks and accusations. The drinker, having no memory of the event, suspects that they are the target of exaggeration and pettiness. The plea of 'I don't remember' soon wears thin. Eventually it sounds like a convenient excuse, another means of denying what needs to be confronted.

Other problems can come with blackouts. Amnesia is no defence for the drinker who wakes up in a police cell. Many alcoholics know the dread of checking their mobile phone to see whom they have phoned the night before, or the confusion that hits when they wake up with a new bedmate. On the other hand, the drinker can minimise the fear, threat and nastiness that they have caused because the incident is only a blank space in their memory.

Repeated blackouts reinforce delusion and the gulf between the family's experience and the drinker's. Both become more isolated in their confusion.

The addicted person believes their excuses and is sure that their reactions are entirely justified. There is an inability to see the mess that is being defended. Judgement is so impaired that they are full of self-delusion and bereft of self-awareness. Both the addiction and the denial of it fuel each other. Denial, like dependency, is progressive. Many people can suffer the loss of their relationships, job, driving licence, good health, and even their freedom through their substance use, and yet maintain the belief that alcohol and drugs play no part in their loss.

The irony of this is that the dependent person can present to professional services such as doctors and mental health teams in the full belief that the main problem is, for example, depression, anxiety, stomach ulcers or marital problems. The further irony is that the person may end up on benzodiazepines, anti-depressants, stomach medication or in relationship counselling. This can reinforce the belief that their substance misuse is, at worst, merely a response to other problems rather than the cause of them. It allows the dependent person to believe that they are improving their situation while the drinking or drug use continues. The further contradiction is that no medication or therapeutic treatment for other issues can be effective while the substance use continues.

Denial is a difficult block to penetrate. It has been unconsciously constructed over the drinking/using lifetime. For some it is a complete lack of understanding that there are now problems; others admit that there are problems, even serious ones. However, missing in both is the realisation of the extent of the destruction. For recovery to happen, the extent of this destruction must be recognised, accepted and absorbed. The perceived reality of the addict and actual reality have grown very far apart. Bringing these together can be a shocking experience. It is a complex and threatening undertaking for the dependent user.

When addiction, with all its defences, is confronted, resistance is usually the automatic response. Therefore its honest exposure, whether through addiction counselling, group work or family intervention, must be done carefully and supportively. As the dependency progressed, those who cared about the addicted person were not similarly protected from its consequences. Supporting these others to articulate their experience can be a powerful tool in opening up the addicted person to the reality of their situation.

Unfortunately, family members often come to distrust their own experience and their own feelings in the midst of this situation. This is where it must be recognised that these people have a right to access support for themselves because they too have a vital need for recovery. Acknowledging such experience, allowing their feelings and providing an understanding of the addictive process are hugely important.

Until this point we have focused on what happens to the drinker or user as their addiction deepens. This has highlighted the obvious consequences for those who are living alongside it. However, we will now shift to a deeper and more personal exploration of how these consequences set in and become a part of those individuals who are affected by another's addiction.

3. What is Happening to Me?

> There is no lonelier place than living with someone who
> is addicted. I was so afraid and confused. In the end
> it was me who changed, and that was what made the
> difference. (Greta)

In order to examine the impact of addictive behaviour
on close relationships, it will be useful to draw on the
experience of those who have lived with a loved one's
addiction and who have managed, with effort, to put their
own lives back in shape. The next three sections give a
sense of what it can be like to live with the addiction of a
partner, of a child and of a parent. The people described
below are real people. Having achieved a distance from
and an understanding about the whole addictive process in
themselves and in those they lived with, they can look back
at their lives and reactions. Looking back, it is easier to see
the actions, helpful and unhelpful, that they carried out as
they struggled to make changes in their circumstances.

Living with a partner's addiction

When people commit to love each other 'in sickness and
in health', they generally do not anticipate sickness in the
form of an addiction. This is a bewildering and frustrating
condition for all involved with it. Partners can feel they are
witnessing a grossly selfish preoccupation; at other times
they suffer a vague but powerful sense of there being
something deeply amiss, but become confused about the
cause. One of the most painful consequences for a partner
is the powerlessness they feel. When a loved one is sick the
instinct is to care and to access all available help.

In addiction it appears that when help is offered it is often refused, and only when the sufferer is ready to accept help can any real change take place. However it is hoped that the following case study will illustrate that partners of addicted people have more control than they have come to believe.

Greta and Mark

His brother told me when we were engaged that Mark was an alcoholic. I didn't believe him. I didn't even know what that meant. There was no big drinking in my family. I loved Mark deeply. We had plans. It took a long time for me to realise that he was in trouble, but the signs were there. He spent our wedding day sitting at the bar. I told myself that it was normal for him to be out most nights of the week with his mates. I believed it was normal because he said it was – even when he sometimes didn't come home at night. If he stayed in he drank and shared his beer with me but I couldn't keep up with him.

When the first two children came along I knew it wasn't right that I was so alone and so lonely. This wasn't how my sisters were living and I was jealous of them. I tried to explain what was happening but it was as if they didn't hear me.

Then the lies started. The money never added up. He pretended to make phonecalls to his boss, shouting down the phone that his money was due – in fact he'd already spent it on drink. I played detective. We were always trying to keep one step ahead of each other. He became arrogant and bullying. He punched walls and broke doors. The children were terrified of him. He apologised – and then went back to drink. When he bought me flowers I knew he had been drinking, or was about to. He blamed me: his drinking was due to the stress of a bad marriage. I knew in my heart that it was his drinking that was wrecking the marriage. His family believed his story that I was nagging and demanding. He believed it too. Even I wondered at times.

Mark the Husband became Mark the Drinker. He thought he needed drink to be likeable and companionable. In fact it took all this away from him. It took me fifteen years to decide that I needed to escape from the man he had become.

There are threads in Greta's story that echo from so many people who live with an alcoholic. The self-doubt and loneliness are clear. Despite seeking support, Greta could not find anyone close to her to accept that she was struggling. Even when the signs of addiction became undeniable, she followed the tendency to endure the situation until change seemed impossible.

Greta has gained huge insight into what was happening to her. The critical feature in how she describes herself during this experience is that she can do this now in retrospect, from the standpoint of her own recovery. In the midst of living with addiction Greta did not know what was going on. This is how she explains it now:

I find it astounding that it took me fifteen years to understand that addiction was the problem. The realisation of this was so gradual and slow. Mark was not ticking all the boxes that amounted to 'alcoholic' as I understood it. I wish I had listened more to my own instinct.

There were good times but fewer of them as time went on. In fact I came to dread it when things seemed to be going well. Then I knew the next bender would be coming soon. He protected his drinking by being good to me so that I could have no right to complain when he did go drinking. I tried so hard not to rock the boat, to be kind to him so that he might stay sober. Of course it never lasted; when he started drinking he was cruel and nasty. He knocked me off the pedestal he'd put me on.

When he was on a bender I couldn't sleep for worry about where he was and what he was doing. When he wasn't drinking he was uptight and irritable. All night my head would be busy anticipating the next binge and what would come with it. I was also managing two babies and a house on my own. This was where all my energy was going. I was short-tempered with the children. I was literally sick with worry at times. Mark told me I enjoyed being a worrier and should lighten up, that everything would be all right. There were times I felt relieved – even grateful – when he came quietly home after a drinking session and there were no arguments.

It could have been worse – there was no physical violence, and in all my checking up I could find no sign of an affair (apart from the one he was having with alcohol).

The disappointments kept coming. I became very bitter and often felt a raging hatred towards him. I was remote from him and I was unhappy. I felt I was in this on my own and the only closeness I had was with my children. I made sure they looked well. I was afraid that people would see that I wasn't coping. I felt like such a failure and put my efforts into hiding this.

We had no connection emotionally or physically. I moved into my daughter's room. At first I got verbal abuse for this. Then he seemed to stop caring. I gave up trying to talk to him about his drinking because he always twisted the discussion into fault-finding with me. In fact, he got really controlling and possessive. He was the one going out on the rip and yet he was accusing me of flirting with other men. Even if I'd had the energy to just go out with my family it wouldn't have been worth it. He would interrogate me and accuse me of being up to all sorts of things.

I think I gave up and just got on with coping. I totally lost sight of myself. I didn't realise how damaged I had become. All the things I thought were wrong with me and my family were because of addiction. I wish I had understood this earlier.

'Getting on with it' is often the safest course for families to settle in to. They manage the crises as they arrive and avoid threatening the status quo. Fun and socialising within the family as well as outside it can gradually fade away. Like Greta, we get more hurt and tired and often more bitter; we lose our compassion.

There is an irony in how addiction becomes expressed by both the addicted person and those closest to them. Both become irritable, defensive and angry. Both suffer the delusion of hoping that this is just an unusual episode in their lives, a phase that will pass, that it is not characteristic behaviour. Both retreat from those who care about but do not understand them. Both can become entrenched in a pattern that allows the problem to continue. Repeated stress and unpredictability will damage any individual. The very nature of addiction is divisiveness and confusion. There is a great deal of feeling but it is often explosive or distorted in its expression.

Trying for change

When addictive behaviours continue, and no amount of condemning, punishing and disapproval makes an impact, then other tactics will come into play. In an effort to make displeasure clear, after having shouted it from the rooftops and having it ignored, the silences will take place and the atmosphere will resound with silence rather than words. This is perfectly understandable and worth a try for one of the two responses it will bring about. There will either be apologies, probably including some excuses, and a promise to quit the offending behaviour. This may resolve the issue – for a while at least. Or there may be a very negative reaction: with or without an argument the tension and frostiness may be construed as a reason to resort to the very behaviour that caused it.

Greta met it often in the early days of Mark's excessive drinking:

> I felt so angry at his constant outings to the pub that I couldn't speak to him. He'd provoke me into shouting and then say that it was no bloody wonder he drank and that he was getting out for a bit of peace.

Greta tried to remove the substance that she saw as causing the problems. She developed the hunting skills of a bloodhound to uncover the bottles hidden, for example, in the garage, the cistern and round the back of the fridge. The result was a furious and humiliated alcoholic who either stormed out or became more ingenious about his hiding places. In Mark's mind, Greta and her interference soon came to represent the problem rather than his own behaviour around alcohol.

To alleviate the backlash Greta tried the appeasing approach. In the hope that by providing a controlled amount of alcohol in the home, Mark might settle for four cans of beer and a night in the house, she duly served the first of them with his dinner. In Mark's addicted world this translated as approval of his drinking. The expectation of beer with his dinner soon became a demand. By the time the fourth can was finished and the familiar warmth was taking hold, Mark was planning how he could access a half bottle of whiskey to wash it down.

Greta tried bargaining with Mark. If he would stay off drink during the week she would not complain about his drinking at the weekend. This strategy failed at a spectacular rate for several reasons. It relieved Mark of responsibility for his problem drinking. Greta was now declaring him fit for drinking sessions. The amounts and the consequences could now be laid at Greta's feet, apparently with her blessing. Now that Mark had lost control of his drinking she tried to gain control of it. Of course, the amounts and the consequences became more serious. The weekend got longer, soon beginning on a Thursday after work. What also became more difficult were the days between the binges. The first few days were often written off as Mark fell casualty to hangovers and withdrawal. His physical and emotional detox was unpleasant to watch. His gnawing impatience for the end of this enforced temporary abstinence was apparent in his irritability and his punishment of Greta for seizing control of the power he had lost over drinking. Eventually he ensured that she was glad to see the weekend arrive so that they could both get peace when he was out drinking. By now he was topping up on most days anyway to offset the worst of withdrawal.

At the same time Greta was performing rescue attempts on Mark's job. Several times she phoned his boss to explain that Mark had the 'flu, or a tummy bug, or an ear infection. She borrowed money from her mother to pay the fine when Mark was caught breaking the car windscreen of someone who had caused him some offence. She told her mother the money was for her daughter's PE equipment. For all her condemnation, Greta was frequently helping Mark to ignore the results of his addiction. The inconsistent messages about this cancelled each other out in Mark's mind. He could sidestep the reasons why he should stop.

Greta was increasingly disgusted with the selfishness of Mark's drinking. In an effort to refocus his commitments she attempted to appeal to his sense of guilt. She begged him to spend time with his children, describing their fears and hurts and quoting many of the examples of when he had let them down. Unable to argue, he argued anyway, accusing her of exaggeration and expecting too much of him. She was too close to the truth and a part of him knew it. He could not accept it and continue to drink as he did – so he did not accept it and shut down the deep discomfort with continued drinking.

How then to break this vicious stalemate? Be absolutely clear that no one can stop addiction except the one who is addicted. But if family members can unwittingly help the addicted person to keep using or drinking, they can also help them to see that it is unacceptable. They need to choose which life they want. The longer this decision is put off, the greater the mess becomes and the harder it is to have clarity about the situation.

When enough is enough

Years of living in this way harm everyone. Sometimes this cannot be repaired in the family unit – but sometimes it can. Despite the length of time and the depth of hurt described above, Mark did attain a good recovery. Greta and Mark have worked hard to achieve a relatively normal and happy life together.

The important truth in all of this is that the turning point came from Greta. It was she, not he, who initiated the changes, and these were difficult to carry through. It is often a major crisis or disappointment that brings this shift. Sometimes it is the addict who realises that they cannot live this way any longer; more often it is their partner who comes to this understanding. It was no big disaster that shifted Greta to this, just another broken promise and the realisation of her powerlessness to change Mark. She simply had 'had enough'. It was Greta's leaving that forced Mark to face the reality of his drinking. Only then did he seriously undertake the work involved in breaking addiction:

> He promised that he would be in the house that morning to take delivery of a freezer I had ordered. I had a part-time job and had to go to work. I heard him crashing in after six in the morning. When I got up he was lying in a mess on the sofa.
> I knew he wouldn't be answering the door to anyone that morning. That's what broke me. At teatime I told him that the next time he came back to the house drunk he would not be getting in. It took five hours for him to try. By then I had sent the kids to my sister's house for the night. I had got my brother-in-law to change the lock and to stay in the house with me. When Mark could not get in he raved and shouted and tried to kick the door in. I phoned the police. I got a barring order put on him and over the next few months he was arrested twice for arriving at the house drunk. I had to change my phone number. It was really frightening. I was worried that he would try to get to me by harassing the children and he did try it once. He was told that he would be going to jail if he did not stay away. In one way I would have been really embarrassed for my family if this had happened, but I also thought it might be a way of getting peace from him and his drinking. For years I had wanted to put him out but couldn't find the nerve. In the end I was so angry and fed up with it all that it wasn't so difficult.

Four months later Greta took a phonecall from Mark in which he explained that he had been accepted for a residential treatment programme and asked if she would attend as his family support. More for her children than for herself or Mark, she agreed. It turned out to be more than she had bargained for.

I thought that his treatment was about him understanding and stopping his drinking. It was all of that, but it also asked me to examine what had happened to me as a person, at how I had shut myself down and away from the world to cope with his behaviour. I had no idea what I had been through until I talked about it all. It was very painful for both of us, but the relief, understanding and strength that I got from that is still powerful. I'm not sure that I will entirely trust Mark again but I certainly trust myself.

On two subsequent occasions Mark found himself packed off to his mother's house. He embarked on a nostalgia trip to the pub and kept his consumption to a few pints. If Mark wanted to think that he could now manage a few sociable drinks Greta was having none of it. She was absolutely clear about the familiar road that this would take him on and she would not be doing the journey with him. Mark made his choice quickly and swapped the local pub for his local AA group.

It would be simplistic to view this as a happy ending. Fifteen years of alcoholic damage is sure to leave scars on any family. This is not a marriage that has survived without cost. Greta has grown strength in coping with it all but has also come to see that she has paid with other qualities:

During those years I had to become strong to get through it, but I hardened too. I will never let anyone walk over me again. I am left suspicious, not only of Mark but also of anyone who I think would take advantage of me. I get intolerant of that in other people too. I know that I am very strict with my own children. So far none of them have dared to come home under the influence of any chemical – and God help them if they do. There is a distance now between my older sister and me: she dismissed me when I needed her support. She was so caught up in playing happy families in her own life that she did not see that I was sinking. I cannot blame her for missing the signs but she didn't take me seriously when I really tried to explain to her the state my family was in. I suppose I have lost a lot of my softness. I had to. There is still hurt and anger in me, and Mark knows it.

When a child becomes addicted

> *I hated the person my daughter became, but underneath all that anger was a serious worry that I had failed as a parent, like I had a duty now to sort it out. (Jean)*

To witness a child suffering a full-blown addiction is a heart-breaking situation for any parent to endure. Parents are hard-wired to wonder if they are responsible for their children's failings, and this is a tendency that persists into the child's adulthood. It is the most profound parental instinct to protect one's offspring from harm and danger and yet many parents find themselves watching helplessly as addiction destroys the potential and the life of their child.

Teenage years are traditionally difficult – some would say as much for parents as for the offspring. If drugs and alcohol are added to the heady cocktail of hormones, angst, identity crises, infatuations and youth culture, then tensions, arguments and stand-offs are sure to follow.

Often experimentation with substances are secretive activities, carried out – and often recklessly so – within the peer group, away from the disapproval or horror of concerned parents. It can be difficult to know if young people are using drugs or alcohol regularly. The symptoms of regular use – tiredness, lying, moodiness, secrecy and bursts of temper – are symptoms of adolescence as much as they are of alcohol or drug use.

It is often undeniable evidence of heavy regular use, such as finding the drugs or young people repeatedly arriving home drunk, that will alert parents to the situation. Even then it is hard to gauge the extent and severity of the problem, whether they are faced with serious dependency or a passing phase, or the vast range of possibilities between. Certainly, if dependency has set in, the defensive attitude, the withdrawal from family and resistance to help will often be particularly acute in young people. It is more often a parent who will seek support when this is ongoing. This is rightly so: by then most parents will have enforced, without success, a range of disciplinary measures and perhaps the occasional bribery tactic.

At this point parents are generally worn out, despairing, angry and deeply worried about their child. The relationship seems irreparable. There is often a deep-seated worry that they are at fault, and that the ongoing substance use is their failure. Often there is an added sense that the drug use or drinking could have been spotted sooner.

While families, young people and dependency vary in their development, there are common feelings that Jean expresses well in her struggle to deal with her daughter's drug use and drinking.

Jean and Rosie

I had no reason to think that my daughter was going to end up addicted to drugs. I gave her the best upbringing I could. Her father was an alcoholic and I left him when she was five, and that was for her sake as much as mine. Maybe I spoilt her a bit – I was trying to be two good parents to her and her sister. But there were no big problems with her until she was about fourteen.

She became cheeky and defiant. It was like I didn't know her anymore. She was just blatantly disobedient and nasty to her sister and me. She came home drunk a few times when she was fifteen. She was a bit shame-faced for a day or two but that was it. I read the riot act, but it was water off a duck's back. I wasn't keen on her friends but what could I do about it?

Then another parent said to me that the crowd she was with was using drugs. I searched her room. Even I recognised the butt-ends of joints. There were homemade bongs made from lemonade bottles and pen-shafts. When I confronted her she lost her temper, tried to make out that I was in the wrong for snooping around her bedroom. I spoke to a community worker, I got information for her on drugs, I tried to negotiate ground rules and she ignored it all. When she was getting 'nagged' in the house, she just decided that it was much more fun to be out doing her thing with her mates. She'd *just storm out and eventually come back in a state that meant she didn't care what I said. I grounded her and she climbed out the window. In desperation I locked away her clothes and shoes and took her phone. But she always found a way out, usually with the help of her friends. I spoke to her form teacher because they were having problems with her too.*

No matter what I did, she became more and more out of control. I became really worried for her safety and her future. Eventually, in sheer desperation, I let her bring her friends to the house in the hope that she would be less at risk of using other drugs, or getting into dodgy relationships. I tried to make our home a place she would want to be but it was a waste of time. She still disappeared without telling me where she was going. Money disappeared from my purse quite a few times. All this was so unfair on her sister but I just didn't know what else I could do.

Jean spent three years trying every tactic she could to divert Rosie from these behaviours. In the battle of wills Jean was no match for Rosie's addiction. The best she could do was to make it more difficult for Rosie to access her friends and her drugs. Still, Rosie found a way around all the obstacles and became angrier and more creative in pursuing her own path. Jean discovered that drugs are easier to hide than they are to find, and that they are quickly replaced, with the result that Rosie descended deeper into debt to dealers and friends and took to thieving to solve the cash-flow problem. Jean simply could not stop her.

In desperation Jean changed tack. She tried to make her home the place that Rosie would rather be. She bought her the best of clothes, cooked the tastiest of dinners, treated her to the latest computer-ware and electronic gadgets in the hope of diverting her into healthier activities, or at least to keep her in the safer environment of the home. Rosie became an indulged drug-user who now had the best of both worlds. In both her home life and her drug life she was being rewarded with what she wanted. Her drug use increased, and much of it with her friends in the home – which could have left Jean in court for committing the offence of knowingly allowing her premises to be used for the purpose of consuming banned substances. As it turned out, Jean was technically financing much of Rosie's drug use as she sold her iPod and a set of speakers to a dealer. Rosie's anger, nastiness and depressive phases all increased and the situation spiralled into crisis for all of them.

As Rosie sank deeper into dependency, Jean sank deeper into despair. Emotionally and physically they both became unwell, unable to see how exhausted they were. Rosie took no responsibility for it, and Jean assumed all of it:

I questioned everything about my ability as a mother. I wondered if I should have left my husband. I even blamed myself for marrying an alcoholic in case this had been the start of her problem. I blamed myself for having taken on another partner when she was younger. I worried that I had indulged her, or that I should have worked harder at building her confidence. I thought I should have seen the problems sooner and that somehow I could have dealt with it all better. I lost touch with my friends and got into a very lonely place. I backed off from my family who thought I just wasn't being strict enough or that I was exaggerating. I ended up on Diazepam myself and Rosie called me a junkie. She then began to steal them. My younger daughter suffered while all the attention was on Rosie. I was so angry towards her but I could also see that she was a miserable mess who was heading for serious trouble. I can honestly say that I felt like an absolute failure as a mother.

When it gets to this, the parent has lost the confidence and energy to look after herself, much less make difficult decisions about her addicted daughter. When Jean did seek the help of an addiction treatment centre she had all but given up. Rosie was undoubtedly in charge of the house and who came into it. Jean had largely retreated to her bedroom, keeping well away from Rosie and her friends as they commandeered the living areas. The younger girl spent most of her time at her cousins' home. Something had to change, and subtle adjustments were clearly not the answer. Rosie's family simply could not continue to live with her addicted behaviour.

Making changes

There were two questions that Jean had to explore, though it was painful to do so. Firstly, what would happen if Rosie were to continue living at home? Secondly, what would happen if Jean told her to leave? Well aware of Rosie's vulnerability, Jean had to face the worst fears of a parent.

The terror that lay within the answers to the second question had to wait. Jean could not even go there until she had exhausted the first possibility. What was clear to Jean was that she would be no competition for Rosie's addiction. It was getting worse, as it always does, and so were conditions at home. Jean went back to seizing some authority. She banned Rosie's friends from the house, reclaimed the living areas and stopped giving money to her daughter.

The outcome was no surprise. Angrier than ever, Rosie stayed away from the house. The police arrived one day to discuss her arrest on suspicion of shoplifting. Evidence was sufficient only to later secure a conviction against her friend. There were screaming arguments and contemptuous silences. Living there was intolerable even for Rosie. Eventually it was she who forced the second question when she declared that she was going to move out of the house. This was the hardest time for Jean:

It broke my heart when she made that decision. Worse, she was moving in with friends. It could not go well. For a few days I coped by offering practical help – I found a place in supported housing for her and would have paid the deposit. But Rosie didn't want that. She was set on moving into a party-house. I was hit with all my fears for her and I fell apart. I could see it coming: the loss of her future, pregnancy, even prison. I feared she would lose her health, physically and mentally. I imagined that she could end up in enough despair to try killing herself.

Yet I'm still a bit ashamed to admit that part of me was relieved to see her go. Her absence was sore on me. I think I missed being able to pin my anxiety on every crisis she brought to the door. Now I was just worried, without being sure what trouble she was in.

Jean had to let her daughter go. Of course it did get worse. There was a year on probation after she was found in possession of stolen goods. There was eviction and debt. Rosie blamed it all on Jean for putting her out, and gained sympathy from both her peers and some of Jean's. There was the night when Jean took Rosie crying from the doorstep back into her home and the day that she had to ask her to leave again because, clearly, nothing had changed. Two years on, Rosie has had a few part-time jobs and lost them. She suffers from depression and declining health. From what Jean can make out, Rosie has cut down on alcohol and drug use but she has not stopped. There is sporadic contact between them.

I love my daughter deeply but I am clear now that I will not let her addiction destroy her sister and me. I have had to stay so strong against the temptation to rescue her from what she is doing. I know she has to do it herself. I can see things getting worse for her again. Maybe they have to. When she is ready to change I am here for her. I would give everything I have to help Rosie find recovery. Until she is ready I will look after her sister and myself. I will take whatever support I can get for us both.

As yet there is no conclusion to this family's story. What is clear to Jean now is that Rosie's addiction was going to take her to bad places – whether or not she stayed at home. By leaving home, Rosie probably got there more quickly. She is now facing the consequences of her own choices and is solely responsible for her decision to stop or continue with this lifestyle. Jean is ready to help her change if she wants to, rather than helping her continue in this way:

I know now that I am not responsible for my daughter's addiction, but I do have guilt and regrets. I probably should have put her out sooner. Maybe if I had been stricter or if I had looked for support earlier it would not have got to this. Then again, maybe it would. I cannot know this. Right now I just have to do what's right for the three of us. Our family has been through enough.

A note on 'adult children'

Addicted children are not always teenagers. Ageing parents too are tolerating the relentless drinking patterns of offspring in their forties – people who have settled to expect little from their adult children by way of financial or emotional support. They continue to look after them as if they were gruff and irresponsible teenagers, resigning themselves to their emotional immaturity. The drudgery of non-communication becomes the norm and it is always a crisis that brings the weariness of the situation into focus. As time goes on, making changes seems more frightening and impossible. Making change should be considered. It **can** be done.

When a parent drinks too much

> *I thought if I behaved better then Mammy might not drink as much. I tried so hard to make her stop. (Maria)*

Children are, of course, vulnerable. They need protection, love and stability. They are also profoundly loyal, maintaining a deep love and idealisation of parents despite some horrendous disappointments from those in whom they trust most.

We know that many thousands of children in Ireland are currently living with at least one addicted parent. What they witness, how much they suffer and how well they will recover depends on many factors. There are children who see and who are subject to horrific violence and neglect. There are others who have a vague sense that something is amiss, but who will be able to recall a fairly stable home and many happy memories. The range of addicted behaviours and consequences is vast and experiences will differ between families and individuals.

Generally, it is unusual for a child to emerge from an addicted household unscathed when their formative years have been spent there. The effects of mood-swings, inconsistency, unreliability and tension that surround an addicted person seep into the child and others in the home. At best, children learn to expect less and to avoid being the direct target of the emotional maelstrom that frequently tears through their home.

This necessity to rise above the fears and hurts of a parent's addiction is one of its saddest legacies. Children often avoid the worst of the fear, the disappointment and the hurt by tuning out of their own feelings. Some can still immerse themselves in their childhood world of the imagination for much of the time. Inevitably though, adult problems come crashing in.

Parents often cling to the false (but comforting) delusion that their children remain unaffected. There are indeed children who do not see the worst excesses of their parent's drinking or the act of using drugs, but most have suffered from the related behaviours that the addicted person cannot see. That addicted parents love their children is not in question. Of course they do, but this love is inconsistent, often conditional, and secondary to the relationship with the substance they are using. As a consequence, the children of addicted people inevitably question their parents' love for them.

Maria's Mum

When I look back on my childhood – and I generally prefer not to – what I remember most is being frightened. I was the eldest of five. When the arguments started I put the blankets up over the heads of the little ones so that they might not hear it. Both my parents were drinkers, but my mother more so. Often it got physical: she'd shout and insult him until he tried to throttle her to shut her up. When he threw her out she broke doors and windows to get back in. The next day they would happily walk down the street together as if nothing had happened, but I was too ashamed to look the neighbours in the face. As I got older it was me who had to sort out the glazier to fix the glass.

I remember teenage years more because I often got the brunt of it. I was beaten by both of them for things I had never done. I prayed so hard that they would stop drinking and I would have done anything to fix them. But I learnt never to challenge their drinking. That didn't end well for me. I was getting jobs by the time I was thirteen but I never saw the money. I didn't question that it was my responsibility to care for the younger ones, to keep them clean and fed and to sort out their problems. I just learnt to get on with it. I left school as soon as I could even though I was doing well. I had to bring in money and got work in a factory.

I got married young. I always wanted a family so that I could give them everything I never had, especially the safety to talk to me about anything they wanted to. My husband had to put up with a lot. After my father left, my mother would often turn up drunk or abusive to my house, or I'd get a phonecall to go and sort her out. By now I had children of my own.

Another vicious argument when she was coming off drink finished me. I was still getting blamed for all the problems she had and now I was being accused of being superior and having a perfect little life. I went to Al-Anon and then for counselling at the treatment centre. That's when I really got control of my life. I will always treasure the relief of telling all the secrets I felt I'd had to keep all my life. At last someone was asking how I was and making it alright to say what I had been through. It gave me the confidence to believe that I did not have to put up with it any more.

Ben's Dad

It was wisest to be in bed when he came home. We knew in the first five seconds how it was going to go. Strangely, the noisier he was the less we had to fear. That meant he was in a good mood. He was still the life and soul of his imaginary party. It was up to Mam to be a good audience if she wanted the mood to stay jolly. Sometimes, in that mood, he would come up and slobber kisses over my brothers and me and tell us what great lads we were and

*that he would take us fishing at the weekend. I think I was
five the last time he kept that promise.*

*If he came in quietly we knew that there was going to
be trouble. He came home wanting an argument and he
made sure he got one. We'd be hanging onto each other
upstairs because we knew what was coming. We'd feel
sick with fear. The shouting started. I'd pray she wouldn't
shout back. Later I knew that it riled him more if she didn't.
When the shouting stopped we knew he was hitting her.
The night he crashed her against the window I ran down
the stairs and out the door and banged at neighbours'
doors until some man came in and stopped him.*

*When I got older, about nine or ten, I deliberately got
between them. He would throw me out of the way and
Mam would shout at me to go back upstairs but I would
keep coming back. At fourteen I discovered the escape
that alcohol and drugs could give. When I was on drugs I
felt confident and light. I could forget about my father, at
least until I came home. When I was fifteen I marched into
one of their fights and I hit him. I did him a lot of damage. I
know I should probably feel bad but I don't. He didn't beat
her as much after that.*

This is quite an extreme example of what children can
witness. Sadly, it is not the most disturbing of the scenes
we could relate. Boys want to protect their mothers. Ben
took responsibility for trying to protect his mum. Despite
his efforts he could not stop the assaults. He even blamed
his mother for provoking the situation when she argued
back or did not give the right response.

Mary's Dad

*There was no physical violence. I hardly ever saw him
drunk. We did okay financially, and really there was
nothing that would suggest we were anything but a
perfectly respectable family who just kept to ourselves.*

*I hated their arguments – I was waiting for violence
that never came. For me it was my mother who was the
problem. She was stressed out. She was proud; her family
were in another town and she wouldn't have admitted to*

anyone anyway that her husband was a drunk and that she wasn't coping. The only one who knew the problem was me. I listened so much to her contempt for him that I disliked him too. He was just sleeping, or away drinking, or working, or with his mother who could see no wrong in him and who believed he deserved the comfort of his drink for having to put up with my mother.

All this left her like a wound-up spring, and when she unravelled it was me who got it. I spent my childhood trying not to annoy her and being invisible. I was the messenger between them. There was just me, so their secrets were safe. There was never another child allowed in the house, and rarely another adult. His drinking and their problems were 'none of my business', and materially I was well cared for. When he died of pancreatitis I felt nothing but relief. I thought my mother would be happy now, but she wasn't.

That there are three case studies presented to illustrate children's experience of a parent's addiction has been done quite deliberately. Children often take on different roles within a family. Addiction can exaggerate the characteristics of these roles. It can be seen above how Maria adopted the role of mothering and took on responsibility that was unfair to her. She protected her younger siblings and escaped the family home as soon as she felt able to do so. Even so, the trait of being carer to others has never left her. Ben tried to protect his mother and eventually found his escape in the altered state that drugs offered. Mary escaped negative attention by being 'invisible' and by concentrating on her mother's emotional state rather than on her own.

In these cases we cannot ask what they, as family members, could have done differently. They were children. They tiptoed through their childhood along the only route they could find. It was up to adults to show them a safer route. Due to the power of the family secret that so often accompanies addiction, none of these children were helped. They were distracted and preoccupied with the behaviour of their parents, carrying a shame that should not have belonged to them and a responsibility that damaged the freedom of their childhood.

Ben knew he could have phoned a helpline. He thought about it sometimes:

I didn't dare. What if I'd been caught making the phonecall? What if they wanted to know where I lived? I thought they could track the phone number. I couldn't see past the violence that would come if my dad found out I'd made a phonecall like that. I thought about saying to a teacher. I was always in bother at school – I couldn't imagine that any of them would want to help me, and I hated them all anyway. I was vaguely aware that Social Services could come in and then I would have felt responsible for splitting up the family. I wondered if things would be worse or better for us then. I did fantasise about being sent to a nice family where I had loving parents and I was happy. But I didn't believe in it. No, I wouldn't have dared.

In these case studies it is clear that the life being lived out by those around the addicted person is unfulfilling and unhealthy. The characteristics of real relationship and communication – honesty, understanding, listening – are not present. It is not that addicted people are inhuman, but their humanity is corroded by dependency. Driven by the need for the next drink, fix or binge, other obligations become obstacles that have to be brushed aside. Sadly, this includes family and children. It is a measure of the powerfulness of addiction. The rejection felt by the family members is big. The continuing drinking and using cynically assert that they don't matter. Yet this is not the full picture. It may be helpful now to listen to Mark as he describes the state he was in at the time, and to hear how the locked-in feelings of guilt, disgust and isolation spiralled into more drinking.

I know now that I behaved as if I had no interest in my children. I know that I let them down and lost touch with how they were doing. I had no idea what was going on with them because I was such a mess myself. But it isn't true that I wasn't aware of this. I didn't know how bad it was because I had so many blackouts, but I knew my drinking was hurting them. I don't blame Greta for pointing it out but it felt she was twisting the knife. Inside I felt disgusted with myself. The problem was that I did feel so bad about it. When I realised I'd let them down again I couldn't deal with the guilt that was rising up. I knew I couldn't make it up to them, and I knew I wasn't finished with drink so I did what I always did when I felt disgusted with myself – I went and did more drinking. I know that wasn't how Greta saw it because I just turned on her when she said these things. The worse I felt the more I drank and it just got worse for them too. Understanding this and hearing it from my kids has been the hardest part of my recovery.

It is not true, then, that alcoholic and addicted people have no idea that they are in trouble. At the very least they are aware of their own sense of misery: 'not happy with it and not happy without it'. They become victim to their own sense of helplessness, and the unhappiness deteriorates into the self-pity that is so characteristic of addiction. They miss the details; they forget, minimise or displace the consequences of their addiction onto those around them. They become painfully isolated and lonely. The absurdity of addiction kicks in, that the very substance that led them to this is the crutch they turn to for coping with the pain that it has caused. When everyone else is angry and distanced, when the ordinary satisfactions in life have disappeared, the alcohol or drugs are the one constant, promising – if not delivering – some relief. Surrendering this leaves them with nothing but the mess they have inflicted on themselves and on everyone around them.

4. The Things We Do to Cope

What not to do

We got some sense of Greta and Jean's desperate attempts to rein in their loved ones, and why these efforts did not work. Their labours are not unusual for people in this situation. There are standard devices that are commonly used within alcoholic families and we will look at them now. While being acutely aware of individual situations, we will set out methods that are unhelpful in dealing with addiction as well as approaches that can ensure that the addictive behaviour has to be faced by the one caught in it.

Hiding the problem
While shame becomes deeply embedded in the psyche of the addict, it also affects the wider family. This is no surprise. We live in a society that has celebrated heavy drinking over many centuries. We have worn it as part of our cultural identity: we are the hard-drinkin' fightin' Irish who are fond of the jar and up for the craic. Yet when we cross that line into a habit that is threatening and out of control we are silenced with embarrassment. Alcoholism is outed only in the later stages by the effrontery of the 'winos' on the streets that can no longer maintain the decency needed to keep it hidden from public display and whose craic has turned sour. Likewise with drugs. Before the smoking ban it was not uncommon to see smokers puffing joints in the corners of pubs. Cocaine is accepted at many parties and between friends. Those who get addicted spoil the party for the others by displaying its most improper side effects. There is little public sympathy when dependency creeps in.

So we, as family, hide this most embarrassing condition from public censure. Often this requires us to hide ourselves away as well. It is best to keep our friends away from the home lest addiction declares itself to them offensively. Our lives become centred around the behaviours and crises that addiction brings and we draw back from other social activities. We have little common ground for friendly conversations. We are tired, distracted and edgy and withdraw from the company of others. We fear the judgement of our relatives and keep them at bay. Consequently we develop the symptoms of guilt, isolation and loneliness that are also felt by the addicted person. It becomes progressively more difficult to reach out to people as our situation worsens.

Telling lies

The alcoholic or addicted person is not the only one who resorts to lying, minimising and making excuses. We saw it earlier when Greta lied to Mark's boss about why he was missing work. Greta was trying to protect his job and their income. Looking back on it now she can see it from a very different angle:

> It turned out that his boss had a fair idea that his drinking was a problem. Unfortunately he didn't do much about it. Mark was a good worker so he got away with a lot. In the early days they used to go to the pub together after work. That didn't happen so much after a few years because the boss couldn't keep up with him and Mark could get very tetchy on the drink. What I didn't know though was that Mark had got a few warnings from him to clean up his act and sort it out. It wasn't formal warnings but it shows that Mark didn't hide it as well as he thought. One of the worst things that could have happened for me was that Mark would lose his job. Now I wonder if that might have been the crisis that would have brought him to his senses. As long as he had the job he had easy drinking money and the belief that he was keeping it all together.

Greta thought she was protecting her family and its income, as well as their reputation. In fact she was protecting Mark's drinking, lying to his employer and helping him to take his hangovers to bed or steady them with further drinking. So long as Mark's employer could be convinced that Mark did not have a drink problem, then Mark could be convinced of it too. As it was, Mark lost his home before he lost his job, and it was that which forced him to face the reality of his addiction.

Cleaning up the mess

Addiction leaves a mess in every possible sense of the word. In almost every addicted family there is at least one person striving to maintain some sense of order and normality. Greta tidied up the beer cans and bottles. Jean, for a time, cleared up the ravages left by Rosie's friends in the kitchen and living room. Maria got windows replaced and cleaned up the sick on the stairs. Ben's dad, unknown to him, had his bed changed almost daily by Ben's mother so that he would have one less thing to get embarrassed and angry about.

Families have paid fines, covered up, gone to great lengths to keep a relative's name out of the newspapers and even helped do the addicted person's job for them. They have seen their loved one drive away drunk or high on drugs and they have not alerted police lest the driver lose their licence. It all amounts to preventing the addicted person from seeing the extent and consequences of their lifestyle. What reason, then, do they have to stop?

Making empty threats

When dependency worsens and nothing changes for the better, a strong instinct will bring a partner or parent to consider drastic action. This is a good instinct. Do not ignore it. Nothing now will change until you – or catastrophe – changes it. It is best not to wait for disaster. In forcing the situation to its absolute crisis point, the choice is undeniably before the person who is the source of it all. It is the decision that both Greta and Jean eventually took and it was done in full knowledge that it might end in a different kind of failure.

It was especially hard for Jean because she had to face her deepest fears for Rosie:

Every time I made a threat that I did not keep, Rosie lost even more respect for me. The boundaries were unclear for both of us. At the time when I knew she would have to leave I felt as if I was losing Rosie forever. In truth I had lost her a long time ago. Worse, I felt as if I was also losing all hope for us as a family and for Rosie's future. I knew things would probably get worse for her before they got better, and they did. They had to. Actually, I have more hope now that she has moved out because I am stronger. I could help her now. I was confused, angry and exhausted when she was with us.

Losing sight of your own needs

Addiction demands attention from everyone around it. It destroys the persons it infects and brings chaos and damage that family members are inevitably left to deal with. This damage is relentless and progressive. Families expend energy in anticipating and acting on this chaos when they have nothing left to give. This is worsened by the hurtfulness and anger meted out by the addicted person. Despite all the self-doubt, loss of confidence and exhaustion being suffered by family members, they doggedly persist in their efforts to lessen the damage and maintain some sense of normality around them. Addiction ensures that family members are cut off from the very support they need most. In times when they are most in need of friendship and care they gradually retreat from it.

While addiction becomes the focus of the addicted person, and this person in turn becomes the focus of the family, no-one else's needs are met. They lose sight of their own strengths and qualities and, like the drinker or user, cease to develop in themselves. There is no fun, relief or enrichment. Life closes in. There is nothing to restore or nourish the emotional fatigue. After years of self-neglect there is then nothing else in place to turn to and the desolation is heightened. This is when people give up and resign themselves to putting up with it all until disaster or tragedy ends it.

Like any addicted person in recovery, family members also need to build a life beyond the focus on addiction. At the point of exhaustion this seems an impossible task, but support and other interests will be the lifeline that pulls people out of the spiral of living with another's dependency.

All of the above scenarios are real, the experience of individual people far from unique. Hopefully, if sadly, you can identify with at least some of the experiences and feelings that these people describe. The case studies raise important questions and we will explore them in the next chapter. Principally the issue of what these family members did to change their situation merits consideration. What happened to the drinker/user, and crucially, what happened to the loved ones who were dealing with it? What does the experience of living with addiction do to others, especially to children? Are there right and wrong ways of coping with it all? How much do you take responsibility for another's addictive behaviour?

These are not stories that necessarily lend themselves to happy endings, and most definitely not to simplistic resolutions. Rather they involve difficult choices that require great strength in carrying them out without the certainty of knowing that they will bring about the desired conclusion. They also require a very courageous willingness to make changes at a point where family members feel bereft of courage, energy and self-belief. The people above did take on their situation in ways that, after much soul-searching, seemed right for them. They did not always make the best judgements, but they kept working at it to change their lives and themselves in the process.

What to do

Addiction by its nature is a loss of control. It has been lost by that person who has the condition of dependency and you cannot find it and reinstate it for them. Do not exhaust yourself by trying to do this. It is an impossible task.

Try not to become embroiled in that person's addictive behaviour or you too will be consumed by it. Turn the focus back onto yourself and how you are. Allow yourself your feelings, however negative they might seem, and allow yourself to share them. Reach out for support and talk about what is happening in your home. Keep in touch with normality by keeping links to the world outside your door. Otherwise you will retreat and shame and resentment will build – much like for the one who is addicted.

Protect your children from the damages of addictive behaviours, certainly, but do not protect the addicted person by denying the children the understanding of what is wrong. They do not need details but they need to be heard and they need to understand their feelings too. It is better for them to know that their parent has a problem with alcohol or drugs than to remain confused and hurt, wondering if the stress and arguments are somehow their fault. Better that they say what might be hard for you to hear than to have them shut down or stay out, not learning how to cope with emotions they are well entitled to have. Help them to understand that the damage is being driven by the addiction rather than by the person that they love. Explain that addiction hurts the person who is addicted. Tell them gently that you too are hurt by the other's addiction. This is not betrayal; it is allowing the children to have the closeness, trust and support that they desperately need. You can do this and yet keep strong for them; it is not the same as putting up a brave front. Brave fronts hide the truth but not the underlying stress. Brave fronts eventually come crashing down. Children will understand your hurt better than rants, tempers and frightening, unexplained mood-swings.

The best guide you have in coping with such a situation is your own values system. Deep down you know what is right and wrong for you and those close to you. It is vital that you retain your own values while the addicted person is progressively losing theirs. The earlier you adopt this stance the better so that you are less likely to become weakened by a pointless effort to fight or control another's dependency. Rather, you need to build your strengths, reaching out to others for some affirmation and support.

This may be found among family or friends, or it may be found in Al-Anon, Nar-Anon or your local addiction treatment centre and counselling services.

Ultimately, the choices you make in dealing with a loved one's addiction can only be made by you. No doubt you will receive plenty of advice, much of it conflicting as others expect you to react in certain ways. Yet only you can understand entirely what you are going through. Trust your instinct. Some people leave the drinker or user; other people have them leave the home. Some families choose to stay together, but this should be done very carefully if the damage is to be minimised. Be aware that this person's primary relationship is with the substance, not with you or anyone else in the house. You are likely to be viewed either as an interference or as someone who can be manipulated into helping that relationship to continue. Sadly, you are in store for a great deal of frustration and hurt unless you can pull back from these two possibilities. Live your life; care for yourself and those in your care. Do not be a third party in the relationship between your loved one and their addiction. It is a toxic partnership that in the end is lethal. Your loved one will either become chronically ill, physically or mentally, or they will make the decision that it has to stop. Your decision to stop enabling or fighting the addiction can help them make that decision. Stay consistent.

5. Enabling the Recovery of a Loved One

Reading through the case histories, it is clear that in the situation of the two adults there was no clear plan on how to handle what was going on. Life became reactive. At one level they had to work incredibly hard to adapt, manage and survive, and yet at another level they felt they were standing still. There was no real change. Eventually, in Jean's case, Rosie made the decision:

> *It broke my heart when she made that decision ... Her absence was sore on me. I think I missed being able to pin my anxiety on every crisis she brought to the door.*

For Greta,

> *For years I had wanted to put him out but couldn't find the nerve. In the end I was so angry and fed up with it all that it wasn't so difficult.*

Each of them in their own way were overcome by circumstances. The change arose out of the exhausted muddle of their lives. Frustration built and forced events to their crisis-point. Jean persisted in her efforts to protect her daughter until it was Rosie who packed her bags and left. Greta's action was impulsive and explosive, though ultimately positive in its outcome. There is, though, another line of action, which is real decision-making. It is different and comes from recognising what is happening to oneself and to the other person, and proactively planning what needs to be done. It involves a considered, serious and open discussion with the addicted person and it is referred to as an intervention.

Making an intervention

'Intervention' is one of those terms that has settled into the language of addiction treatment. It sounds full of its own importance, like a procedure whose workings are the sacred ground of professionals. As in so much of addiction treatment and counselling though, an intervention comes from the same sources: getting clear and honest about what is happening in you and what you want to change. It is one step further – it is getting clear and honest with the addicted person.

An intervention is a calm and honest appraisal of the real impact of a person's addiction on themselves and others. Family are usually the best placed people to do it. At this stage though, family relationships can be fractured and broken. Significant others, for example, a close friend and/ or a fellow worker who knows about the drinking or using, will be important in helping convince the addicted person that the damage is real. It is not the family ganging up against them.

An intervention must be prepared with care. Two essentials must be understood by the people who will initiate it. The first requirement is a good understanding of addiction. If you have read and considered the information in the first two chapters of this book, then you should have a solid foundation in knowing how addiction operates.

The second key understanding you must have is of yourself. What are your feelings towards addiction, towards the person who is addicted, towards yourself and how you too might have changed? What are your motives for intervening? An intervention that is inspired by anger, contempt or frustration will fail: a negative starting point will ensure a negative outcome. What are your expectations from this process? Who should you trust to be with you in this discussion – what is their understanding, their motive, their hope?

An intervention is undeniably a confrontation, but it should not be an onslaught of revenge or an attack on the addicted person. This is why understanding yourself and

your motives is critical. Untangle your feelings first. Talk
them through with someone who will listen well. Take
responsibility for your own reactions. Vent your disgust
and hurts around addiction and get past them. Get to
the person that you care about, the person beneath
the addiction. We hope it has been clearly explained
throughout this book that addiction protects itself. When
attacked, its defences will mount immediately. This is why
your intervention must come from the position of care
for this person. It is possible to be caring, compassionate
and honest while still being firm about your intolerance of
addiction itself.

Recovery is about recovering the person, not removing
the addiction. Addiction will always be part of that person's
being. The hope is that it can be exposed, understood and
disempowered. But first the addict has to see it clearly. The
discussion has to focus on the addiction as the problem
rather than the person – they are already full of shame and
failure no matter how deluded they are (as we saw from
Mark's words). If the goal of an intervention is to make
them feel worse, they will certainly flee to the only thing
they think can ease it – the substance itself – and retreat
from the source of their pain, now perceived as you.

Support the person but expose the addiction and its
effects. An intervention provides another good reason why
your own recovery is paramount. If you have not accepted,
expressed and worked through your own feelings, you
will take them into the intervention with you and will
likely cause further anger, hurt and resentment between
you. This is true of anyone taking part and you should not
undertake it alone. Be clear about why you feel as you do.
Be clear on how addiction has changed the person that
you love, or loved. Be clear about patterns of behaviour,
including those that happened during blackouts. Do talk it
through first so that you can acknowledge to this person
the better part of them, the decency that the substance
has stifled, the values they held and the ways in which
addiction has corrupted them. The aim of an intervention
is to dismantle the delusion that allows that person to

continue their destruction. You want to achieve a setting out of the truth, without recrimination or judgement; otherwise the addicted person will hear only the recriminations and none of the truth.

Obviously an intervention would be pointless while the person is drunk, high or in the throes of a bad withdrawal. Neither is in the midst of a crisis the time to act, but the undeniable aftermath of one can be an effective starting point.

Setting the atmosphere, then, both in your head and your approach to the other person is vital. Be aware that like any of us who could be confronted with our lies, our shameful secrets, the harm we may have done, the addicted person is sure to feel embarrassment at such exposure. It is inevitable and can only be lessened by balancing the positive aspects of that person against the damage of addiction.

Experience will tell you that confronting addiction is met with a backlash. It is why the basis of an intervention genuinely comes from care and concern, an awareness of the addicted person's pain as well as your own and that of others. It must also be carried out with the authority of your belief that this situation is no longer tolerable. You will probably be met with excuses, pleas and all the defences we listed in the second chapter, but you must hold sure to your experience of their addiction because it is you who can see its reality. Set out that reality: what the effects are for all concerned and what has happened over time. Listen to the feelings of the addicted person and be open about your own. Be clear about the choices you are presenting to them. Assure them of your support, but only to work at overcoming the addiction, not to allow its continuance. Set out the limits of what you can no longer live with and provide them with options for help. Be clear that you care about them deeply but will not endure the condition that is destroying them, as well as you and your family.

The intervention should provide direction. It is hard work clearing up in you and for you what has been happening, and making decisions and resolutions about it. It is best to do it with the support and knowledge of the whole family (although you may find in some cases that support might not be given). Only do it when you are fit and ready to do it. It is a serious act.

Leave them with the clear choice to continue with the drinking or using, or to begin the process of taking the support needed to work at recovery. Leave them to make a decision – but do not allow decision time to drift. If they do not come to a clear decision, then the choice, unfortunately, must lie with you.

Coping with relapse

Recovery is seldom a one-off event. More often it happens in steps. There can be setbacks. There can be further bouts of drinking or using. These steps can be either a moving on to a healthy and complete recovery or they can be a falling back into the old habits. It is important to know this and it is important to know the difference. You will know that difference in the attitude of the user, in how they react to these slips and setbacks. If they are honest and open about the difficulties they are having and willing to address those difficulties, then the setbacks can be fruitful and should not be seen by families as complete regression and failure.

These early months can be brittle. The decisions, attitudes and manner of approach that informed the intervention need to be sustained now. It is vital that people continue to talk and listen to each other. It is also vital that the family member and the addicted person appreciate not just their own difficulties but each other's difficulties as well.

Recovery is often mistakenly believed to be a physical abstinence from the substance in question. This is only the first step. There are some medications that can ease the withdrawal process and assist the physical adjustment. It is the emotional regulation that is so painful and there is no quick way to accomplish it. It is also the breaking of deeply ingrained patterns that were forged to sustain the addiction. AA warns us of 'people, places and things' because they all have associations with the old habits and provide a false promise of fulfilment.

The first immediate test is often the cravings that can hit the user or drinker after physical withdrawal. While they may be detoxified, addiction is still very much present to them. Cravings will ease in duration and intensity if abstinence is maintained and the commitment to recovery is sure, but this is little comfort to someone who feels that 'the very core of you is screaming for a fix, like it's your soul that's rattling and you think you will explode if you don't get the relief you need' (Mark).

Cravings manifest themselves in physical symptoms. The headaches, sickness, tremors and sweating that sometimes accompany cravings are the result not of detox, but of the acute fear, anxiety or even panic that crashes in when access is denied to the substance that the sufferer has come to believe will put their world to rights. Their biggest fear is that they cannot cope, that they will be overwhelmed by the strength of their own feelings. It is not entirely irrational: addiction has ensured that they have not been coping with their feelings for years. Now they must cope with intensely negative emotions. They are frightened of fear, and panic that they might panic, in case they cannot cope with it.

Further complications arise from the long-term use of stimulant drugs. Having been repeatedly forced to produce an abundance of endorphins, the newly detoxified brain will stop producing them. The result is a flatness and a short-term depressive phase that can defeat recovery. The user wonders why they would struggle to maintain a recovery that feels so bleak. It takes time for the brain to learn to react towards the ordinary pleasures of living as well as its challenges. In this respect, body, mind and soul all require time and care to restore some balance, to be healed, to regain some sense of normality again.

This is also true for the family. Family members may struggle with exhaustion, anger and bitterness. These feelings may disappoint and confuse them – they may have expected to feel better more quickly. They often do not express these feelings openly for fear of triggering relapse. They should be clear that it is much better for themselves, and the recovering person, to share how they actually are.

Recovery is an utter change of lifestyle and attitudes. Its success is largely dependent on these factors being thoroughly reassessed and altered from the very start. Determination is crucial, but it cannot be the only source of strength. The desperate want for recovery must be present too, along with the belief that it can be achieved. Mark comments on the early stages of his recovery:

I admitted to myself, at last, that I was addicted. I wanted to stop with all my heart but I did not believe that I could do it. I was angry that I could no longer control my drinking. I was frightened to try stopping, and frightened not to try. Fear overwhelmed me but I kept it to myself. Greta would keep asking me if I was okay. I'd keep saying that I was because I knew that me being sober meant so much to her, but I would keep going back to the drink. I kept promising family members that I would stop. I made it too big an obstacle to get over. I was disgusted with myself, and my family were giving up on me. AA helped me. I stopped for a day, and another, and another. At some point I stopped counting days. I just worked hard at finding peace. I also started to tell Greta when I was struggling. It is over two years now since my last relapse and I am happy to be sober. I know what it is to feel confident and content.

There must be the discipline of putting in place the activities and supports that will help that person to attain a recovery that is content, purposeful and rewarding. Determination on its own will make for a difficult and unsustainable abstinence, as we will see in the following section.

For a person to attain a good recovery they must have strong self-awareness, of what it is they want to recover in themselves and in their lives, and what they must do to make it happen. Nothing will change if they don't work to make it change. Within this there must be a new willingness to explore and open up feelings, and to have the humility and courage to share these with the people who are the closest support.

To be listened to and have our feelings accepted, even if the other does not entirely understand or agree, sustains us, restoring the damage that addiction brings to self-confidence and self-worth. It is a risk rarely taken in the midst of an addicted household where the possibility of rejection or rebuff is too strong. This is true for the family as much as the person in recovery. Healing takes place when we are heard and affirmed, all the more so when all family members can hear and open up to each other.

'Not drinking, but not sober; not using, but not clean'

Within the addiction field, 'professionals' can often use a shorthand phrase to describe a complex state. The above heading is one such phrase. When drinking and using are active and states of intoxication are frequent, not drinking and not using are longed-for objectives. However they are not the main goal. As explained in the previous section, abstinence is only the first step. Recovery, to be maintained, must feel worthwhile.

Sometimes a situation will come about where a person stops using but goes no further. Whereas previously the core objective was to obtain and use the chosen substance, now the core objective is to 'stay off'. As we have seen, this is usual in the early stages of recovery, with both the person and the family members highly conscious of this new state. The difficulty and the trouble is the persistence of this emphasis. The substance still dominates the agenda.

If the addicted person, 'determined to beat this thing', does not grow in understanding of themselves or others, they will find recovery tense and unfulfilling. After the initial 'feel-good' factor wears off, the person may, in a rigid fashion, live out abstinence but find in it no satisfaction, contentment or ease. There is a discontent that is hard to define. The abstinent person believes that they are trying hard, and as long as they do not drink or use then they are succeeding. Life is narrow – reduced to one central point. Fear and pride can make a person endure this for quite some time.

The user is deprived of their coping strategy but does not replace it with new skills. There is no investment in learning about self or feelings. There is no humility to seek support. It is a denial of self and a denial of need. Beneath is the ache of something missing; the drinker or user feels deprived. In place of the substance there is now a growing resentment, anger and self-pity. A person may not drink or use, hell-bent on proving their sobriety, but lives seething with hurts, disappointments and bitterness. The addicted person seeks acknowledgement and affirmation of their achievement. Whatever they get can be insufficient and their resentment deepens. Defences are reinforced with all the perceived slights and misunderstandings that come their way.

Initially a partner or family member may do all that they can to support this effort of 'staying off'. Gradually however there is the stark realisation that the addicted person and their needs still dominate the household. The moodiness, anger, self-pity and blaming are still features of everyday life. Now, though, the cause is more intangible. There are no drugs or drink to focus on. Family members may doubt themselves and become confused as to what is actually going on. As the addicted person says: 'I've stopped – what more do you want?' And yet it felt easier to live with them drinking. In the midst of this, outsiders may comment encouragingly on how well the person looks, what great progress they are making. This is not the reality being lived out by the family. Unsure, they often turn in on themselves; they wonder at their lack of generosity; they take on the negative feelings. They feel as unfree as they ever did but with increased disappointment and bitterness, because change has brought no change.

What to do now then? Firstly there has to be the recognition of what is happening. This may be difficult to achieve without the help of an addiction counselling service. It is a painful experience to meet family members who come to an addiction treatment centre after living like this. They are frequently remote from, or very judgemental about, their own needs, feelings and development. Talking through and understanding these with a professional addiction counsellor should give awareness and insight, and a truer overview of what has been happening and why. Remember what Maria said:

> I went to Al-Anon and then for counselling at the treatment centre. That's when I really got control of my life. I will always treasure the relief of telling all the secrets I felt I'd had to keep all my life. At last someone was asking how I was ...

With the help of the counsellor, the family member can then begin to draw up realistic goals, and, with ongoing support, work at them. As in active addiction, it is vital for the family to 'step outside' in order to gain perspective.

6. Recovery: Change for the Better?

In setting out the nature of addictive use and the host of consequences it brings about, it is also very important to remember that recovery happens. It is important to remember that many human beings who were lost in addiction go on to live their lives more fully and effectively as a result. This is also true for those who have lived with or 'under' another's addiction.

The recovery of self (whatever the outcome for the addicted person)

In a very small number of cases an addicted person will, due to a crisis of one kind or another, spontaneously stop and go on to live and recover well. In the vast majority of cases the addicted person is 'interrupted', as it were. They have to be faced with the reality of what is going on by those who care, or outside circumstances abruptly necessitate the need to do something. In the latter case most people accept with reluctance that they need to act. However, within the treatment setting or AA/NA setting, this can change. The reluctance can give way to a painful, honest acknowledgement, understanding and acceptance. From a position of denial or delusion, they face truthfully the havoc and distortion to themselves and to others. This requires courage and humility. The family members also need courage and humility.

As outlined earlier, the pressures of living with addiction also distort those in contact with it. Accepting that you have perhaps unwittingly enabled the addiction is a hard truth to hear. Also difficult is the letting go of that constant but futile struggle to control it. Where family members are involved in the treatment it is a shared journey. The divisiveness that was so often a feature of family life begins to narrow with a growing understanding of what was happening to each other. This process demands deep personal honesty from all involved.

Facing down the addiction brings liberation and relief. Energies that have been spent in destructive arguments, brooding silences, nagging doubts and ceaseless worrying can now be used positively. Having lived so negatively for so long, the addicted person and family are motivated to move on.

The freedom and gratitude of a shared recovery is a lifetime's work. The tools of honesty, talking and listening, and the clarity around the addictive process that have led to this point must continue to be used. Ongoing work in aftercare groups is offered by many addiction services, and with NA, AA and Al-Anon, the twelve-step programme fosters and develops these qualities. This is crucial help.

But even with such help the balance can be lost. The commitment to recovery can be prioritised over the commitment to family. Greta was relieved when Mark started going to AA. She could see the support and help he got in his recovery. A year down the line her relief had become frustration:

I was an AA widow. I was seeing him less often than I did when he was drinking. There were blazing arguments about this. He said he had to keep working at his recovery but it seemed that it was a recovery that only Mark was benefiting from. Meanwhile I was getting more hurt and yet more bitter about how well he was doing. The rest of us were paying a price for it.

After a relapse and a serious threat to their marriage again, Mark could see his behaviour more clearly. He admits that he was not using his support well:

I thought I had to attend to myself, to work through the steps to ensure a good recovery. In fact the steps are not about self. I was using AA badly. Greta and my sponsor helped me see that, but I could only hear it after I had lost my sobriety again.

There will be ups and downs. Trust is not rebuilt in days or weeks. Old habits and old ways of coping are strong. Patience and perseverance with oneself and with others are necessary. In previous chapters we explained that change in a family affects everyone. This is also true of recovery. Family members had shifted roles and taken on responsibilities in their efforts to adapt and cope. In recovery, the drinker or user needs to 're-enter' the family in the journey towards normality and proper responsibility. In acknowledging this, it is pertinent now to note how this new shift impacts on children.

It can be particularly hard on children. They may have absented themselves from the arguments and tension by getting out of the house. They spent time with friends and in friends' houses. They learnt self-reliance and found their own way through it all. Younger children may have been spoilt to make up for the emotional shortfalls. Suddenly things are changing. The boundaries that parents let dissolve over years are reinstated, often without discussion or explanation. Treats are no longer handed out to keep them quiet or to make up. Again, they can feel alone: both parents appear to them to be very involved with each other. They may feel powerless, betrayed and overwhelmed. A battle of wills becomes the new war. The importance of discussion around this with children cannot be overstated so that they can be helped to find and understand their place in the shifting ground that comes with recovery.

Younger children may adapt more quickly. Their inbuilt tendencies towards affection and loyalty allow the closeness to be re-instated when parents reach out to them with fairness, calmness and, above all, consistency.

Older children may be a little less forgiving. The route back to them may be longer and more arduous. These young people do have a right to understand, to have discussion, explanation and to be allowed their own voice. An admission by parents of past vulnerability and wrong-doing is not a weakness. The weakness was the behaviour itself when the use was out of control. Such admission is an act of trust. Discussion and openness brings mutual trust and may take some time to earn. Older children may even be able to take part in the treatment process and this allows for such exploration to be developed in the early stages.

Mark's children were young when he began his recovery. A key moment arrived with him some months after his last relapse:

> Out of the blue my eldest girl asked me, 'Are you alright now, Daddy?' She was six years old. I saw so clearly how much she had been worried about me, how she had been concentrating on me rather than doing her own thing. She must have been waiting in fear for the benders I took, and when I was coming round from my binges she would try to look after me. She told me that she had been afraid I would leave home – and I did for six months. She had also been afraid that I would die. That wasn't unfounded either because that's where I was heading. She was scared for me and for her mother. Now I see her more relaxed, happy for me to look after her, instead of the other way about.

Mark would be the first to admit that recovery has not brought perfection to his character, because it was never there. What is significant now though is that he and Greta can talk about this. They can sometimes laugh at the unsavoury truths they have found in each other. They may be open to each other's views without the brittle sensitivities that prohibited these discussions when drinking and its aggression were a threat. The work is underway. The gradual exploration of their relationship will continue at a pace that they can both manage. There has been healing. Now there is progression and hope. This, rather than alcohol, is the focus of their relationship.

   Mark understands now that the shift in himself that made the difference in his recovery – and his family's – happened when he slowed down.

Somewhere along the line I started to relax a bit. I stopped obsessing about my recovery – or rather about myself. I started tuning in to Greta's feelings and focused on my children's needs as well as my own. But I am not complacent. I know I have a lot of making up to do and I am glad to be getting on with that. What is really amazing is the pleasure in having normality. When I wake up I am not full of fear. The routines I thought were boring and the expectations that were a pressure on me are now a thankful relief. I am glad to collect my daughter from the club. I will never love supermarkets and shopping centres but now I behave like an adult when I'm there with Greta. I used to be so insufferable there that she was sometimes relieved when I stormed off to the pub.

Now I can have a bad day and deal with it. I used to have bad days all the time – I turned them into disasters and made sure that everybody else suffered too. I don't run away from the small problems that come along. I take them on and start sorting them out. I don't turn a minor setback into a calamity.

Greta is also more relaxed and more sure of herself.

I now expect the best in him rather than the worst. I have my husband back and I am so grateful for that – but I'm not going to keep telling him that he's wonderful because he's only doing now what he should always have been doing. At least now I can talk to him. I don't have to hide our problems from him and we work together on the household stuff. I can say what I think and feel and be listened to, not yelled at. We can even disagree. It's a great freedom to know you can have the odd argument and that you can both get past it. He still has some annoying habits – but then he says I do too! We go out together and we take our children out. The house is noisy with all the normal family stuff. It used to be either silent or loud with us shouting at each other. There is a relaxed feeling to the place now and there is fun too. But I know the signs and so do the youngsters. If he ever starts that huffy, angry, sneaky stuff again he'll be out. Me and the kids will never ever go through that again.

Recovery, then, is not so much a tale of happy endings as a shared journey and continued, negotiated work. Support and open discussion are critical. As this continues over time, and consistency and security return to family life (the person does come home when they say they will; the money has not gone on alcohol/drugs; the good mood of the morning is still there in the evening), a deeper aspect of recovery evolves. Each person begins to believe more firmly in themselves; the ability to trust in one's own strengths and to grow close to other human beings develops. The isolation of self lessens. It is possible now to relate to oneself and to others with more ease.

Greta explains it like this:

> *My life changed as Mark's drinking took over. It changed again when I stepped back from it. It really has been the worst of times and then the best of times. My own recovery started when I decided I did not have to put up with Mark's drinking and all the behaviour that went with it. When I joined in the treatment programme it was just constant revelation. I got myself back. I have got confidence, friends, and a lightness and humour that I hadn't noticed leaving me. I can be silly now and have fun, but I can also cope with whatever comes my way. Getting my husband back was a bonus but now there is so much to my life. This has been a powerful experience. I wouldn't wish what I've been through on anyone, but I have to say that coming through it has been amazing. Life is good again. I had forgotten that it could be. We're doing okay, all of us.*

Let us be clear that not every situation turns out this way. Sometimes people separate because the drinking/using continues and makes it impossible for the partner and/or children to remain. This does not mean that you cannot work at your own recovery. We will look at this in the next chapter.

7. Understanding After the Event

When recovery does not happen

Recovery has not happened for Noel's wife. It seemed that it would. His wife, Betty, did take part in rehabilitation and Noel was very much a part of this. The early months were good and all of them began to believe that, this time, it would last.

At the beginning I didn't see it because what I was looking for was the drink. Something changed and I wasn't sure what it was. There was a remoteness in her. I felt that I was being shut out again. The children sensed it too. They were worried that she was in bed sleeping so much, even when they got home from school. She fobbed me off; rehab had exhausted her. It reminded me not so much of the drinking but of the days afterwards when she was out of it on painkillers to come round from the hangover. Turns out that the relapse was actually on codeine before the drink came back into it.

It was worse than ever now because the disappointment was massive. The children were phoning me at work again. The lies came back. She was more vindictive and nasty than ever. Even though I knew she was more disgusted with herself than we were with her, I began to worry about how I was reacting. There were times that I was so stretched and pushed that I nearly hit her. This frightened me – I knew it could not go on. I knew I had to sort myself and the children out.

Noel recognised that if he did not deal with this situation, if he did not focus on himself and his children, that he would collapse. It was a very difficult time. Accommodation and finances were a practical but crucial issue. Betty's access to the children had to be agreed and carefully managed. There were painful scenes as Betty continued to drink. Noel got through with the support of friends and family and continued to use the aftercare offered by the addiction service. Betty is still drinking, but even though there has been separation, it is not a bitter and acrimonious stand-off but rather a realistic negotiation of what can and cannot happen.

I know that if I had stayed, that Betty and I would have been at each other's throats and that the children would have been caught in the middle of it and nothing would have changed. I couldn't let that happen. I know I did the right thing, but God it's been hard. At times I have cried, the children have cried, we've cried together. We've gradually found a way to manage it. We don't share the drinking. But we share good times together when we can. Betty tries to keep it together at birthdays and Christmas and most of the time she makes it. Even if she does drink, all of us know that it's not our fault and not about us. I suppose we know that deep in her heart she wants to be with us – she just can't seem to manage it. I am sad that we have lost so much of her, but we had to find life for us beyond her. I have good times with my mates and family and I can get on with my work without dreading phonecalls or what's waiting for me at home. As time has gone on I see the difference it's making to the children. They love Betty but they know they can't rely on her. They have me. Things are calmer. If there are problems there's space and time to deal with them. If we'd stayed, none of this would have happened.

Sometimes this resolution doesn't come. People hang in there to the bitter end, hoping and trying to bring their loved one out of the addiction, but are defeated. Death often leaves us with unanswered questions. Psychologists talk of the various stages of grief. It is unusual not to feel some guilt or anger, even when the relationship has been happy and close. However, the powerful range of feelings that an addictive life generates compounds the grief. There is so much conflict felt.

*I accept that my mum died through her own drinking,
but I cannot accept that time and again, all through my
growing up, her drink was more important to her than I
was. I hate her for that, and it eats at me wondering if she
loved me at all. (Hannah)*

Hannah is someone who sought support for herself as her
mother's drinking continued. Early in her own counselling
her mother died. Grief was a confusion of many feelings
for Hannah. Different emotions seemed to contradict each
other. Hannah was in danger of trying to rationalise what
she should feel and negating the need to work through all
the turmoil that was rising in her.

*I was so angry at the start, at my mother for doing this to
herself and for throwing back at me the years I had spent
trying to help her. I was angry with my brothers for giving
up on her but for being there when she died when I could
not be. I missed her terribly; missed worrying about her,
missed getting the crazy phonecalls she'd make when she
was drunk, missed her needing me. I had failed. I couldn't
make her stop. It had been my lifetime's mission to get her
into recovery and she wouldn't – or couldn't – do it. I felt
guilty about the times I'd lost it with her or wouldn't rescue
her from her own disasters. I was angry that I'd spent my
childhood putting up with her and looking after her. She'd
wrecked my life and I kept letting her wreck it. I felt pity for
the pathetic person she became and then I was angry that
I pitied her.*

*I am clearer now. She fought hard against addiction
but couldn't fight hard enough. She got weaker and
more disgusted with herself. She was sickened by her
own shame. It was easier to keep drinking than to stop
drinking. Dying was easier than living. She did let me
down. I am right to be angry. But I'm angry with myself. I
was determined to make her better, but I'm beginning to
see that I hadn't a chance and I shouldn't have been trying
it anyway. But she was my mum and I loved her too. It
doesn't have to make sense. Some time I will be able to let
her go. I will not let her drinking damage me any more. I
want to get a life for me now.*

Hannah grew up focusing on her mother's needs rather than her own. Her own wellbeing depended on how her mother was, and her mother's behaviour became her dominant concern. Her own feelings were suppressed in the demands of coping with her mother's drinking. As she says, 'It had been my lifetime's mission to get her into recovery'. Hannah came to believe that she could only get peace when her mother stopped drinking. It is so clear to an outsider that Hannah surrendered her own life and that it is now a hard struggle to retrieve it. In her mother's death, as in her life, Hannah distrusted the feelings that screamed inside her. Her own recovery could only begin when she accepted the dubious freedom of feeling her own pain, hurt, anger and sadness. Recovery will be a long and complex road for Hannah.

Likewise, the road back for a parent who has lost a child is complicated and painful. Guilt is nearly unavoidable. One of the deepest instincts of a parent is to protect and care for their child. We can see from Hannah how damaging it is when the parent–child relationship is overturned by addiction. This also applies when it is the parent who is left and it is the child who has died. One mother describes how difficult it is to come to terms with such a loss:

I am left with the memories of the last three years of my son's life. We had arguments. We hurt each other. He stole from me and he hit me twice. Sometimes he blamed me for his addiction. He became a monster. I lost the son I had in the years and months before he died. I saw the worst in him but couldn't forget the loveliness I'd known in him in the years before that. The last time I was called to his hospital bed I just saw a vulnerable and helpless human being. Addiction killed my son. I am angry with everyone who sold drugs to him and everyone who failed to save him, including myself. In my head I know that only Colin himself could have stopped this. In my heart I have so much anger and hurt. What am I to do with it? It is two years since he died and I am still trying to understand why this had to happen to my son. I tried everything I could. It's little comfort, but I do know that: I tried everything. I probably still need to believe that the failure wasn't mine. (Beth)

Grief is a very private journey. People deal with it differently. Beth has found that understanding and support have not diminished her grief but have helped her to carry it. She has been able to acknowledge and explore much of her guilt, her anger and her doubts. Part of the journey is her acceptance that she could not change her son.

If you have suffered such loss through addiction, your feelings are not abnormal: they just *are*. There can be relief in talking through them, to give yourself permission to work through the heartbreak and confusion. As a parent, child or partner you did what you considered to be best. You did what you felt to be right for you and your family. You took the options that were available to you to protect yourself and others. You did what you could do at that time. You could not defeat addiction, but you can reclaim your own life. There is no blame in that.

8. A Last Word on Addiction

Addiction unchallenged will, of course, have the final word. It becomes more deeply embedded once it takes hold of a person. It does not change of its own accord; change must come from the people affected by it.

If you are affected by another's addictive behaviour, listen to yourself. Listen to your instinct. If you sense that something is wrong, something is wrong.

It becomes more tangled and complex and more difficult to unravel the longer we wait. Like any other condition, the chances of recovery are greatly increased if treatment is sought in the early stages. By this we are referring primarily to your recovery. Addiction will damage you and your family as well as the drinker or user. The more quickly you can take action and find support for yourself, the less you should have to recover from.

A key principle of this guide for families has been the importance of recognising and coming to terms with your feelings, however negative they might be. In seeking help for yourself you are already weakening the power of addiction by refusing to support it. If you can make sense of what is going on with you, you will be in a much better place to see the addiction clearly and act positively. It is not just the alcohol or drugs that hurt families. It is how the consequences of it are managed. The longer they go being badly managed, the more confusing and destructive the situation will become.

We hope that this book has given you an understanding of how addiction works, how it will change the person close to you and how this in turn can change you. Unfortunately there are no formulae for recovery in addiction. We cannot offer you the certainty that in helping yourself, you can kick-start the desire in your relative to help themselves. It does improve the chances, though. At the very least, even if the other continues to drink or use, you will have minimised the damage to yourself and those under your care. One of the most disruptive factors in children's lives is living with relentless tension and constant disharmony between partners. Addiction is the family illness, but you can limit its damage.

Help is out there. Seek the support you deserve. Seek it as early as you can, when your instinct signals the first inkling that dependency is at work. In exploring the situation you will ensure that there will be less hurt for everyone involved.

Useful Numbers

If you have any concerns about a relative's drinking or drug-using, speak to your GP, who can refer you to local services, or telephone Northlands for contact details of an addiction service in your area. Northlands can be contacted on 028/048-71313232.

Central numbers for the AA fellowship are as follows (these helplines will give you contacts and details of meetings in your area), as well as helplines for children, whatever their concern:

Alcoholics Anonymous Dublin	01 8420700
Alcoholics Anonymous Belfast	028 9043 4848
Narcotics Anonymous Dublin	087 1386120
Narcotics Anonymous Belfast	078 1017 2991
Al-Anon (for family members of alcoholics) Dublin	01 8732699
Al-Anon Belfast	028 9068 2368
Nar-Anon (for family members of people addicted to drugs) Dublin	01 8748431
Nar-Anon Belfast	030 09991212
Childline Ireland	1800 66 66 66
Childline UK	0800 11 11

A list of accredited addiction counsellors can be found on the website of the Irish Association of Alcohol and Addiction Counsellors: www.iaaac.org.